ISBN-13: 978-1515145851

ISBN-10: 1515145859

## Cover designs

Eventually I decided to go with the template that the publishing web service provides. It shows my drawing of a character looking at a strange skeleton. You can find the original drawing named "Look at you" here http://kangghee.deviantart.com.

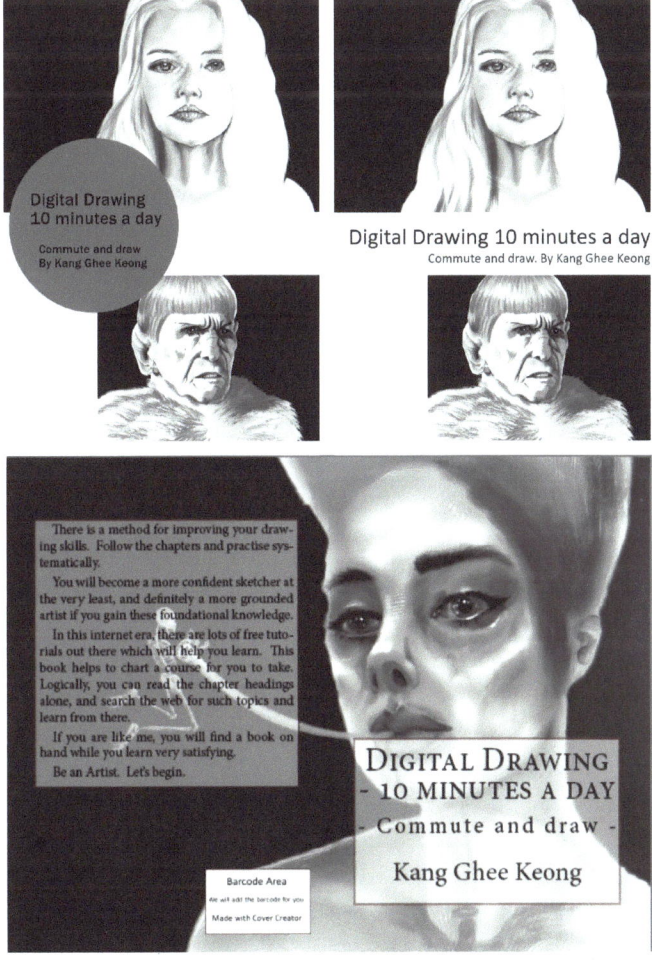

# DEDICATION

This book and all the thoughts put into it is dedicated to my wife, children, parents, friends, brother and sisters, in blood and in-law.

Like a song in my head, "…you are always on my mind…".

# ACKNOWLEDGEMENTS

My wife Ee Hua deserves the most praise, for enduring a husband who changes life directions in seemingly overnight fashions. Love you dear.

My parents are definitely doting, allowing me to try my hand at any passion I have, at any moment in life. Thank you papa and mama. That includes my father-in-law.

My children for lovingly enduring a father figure who seems to be no role model at all! Or perhaps this father leads by example demonstrating how to try everything in life. The lack of consistency might not be good for children's growing years though. Hm… hope you guys grow up well. Crossing my fingers. Love you all.

My brother and sisters, in blood and in-law, who always close one eye to my randomness, and just give my family, wife, children, and me, any support you can afford us. Thank you dears.

My friends, you are not last in my list, just that the heaviest weight is borne by you all, always supportive, always helping to push me along whenever I need it. I am only as good as the people I surround myself with. So I am glad to have been among giants like you.

Some special artists deserve praise as well. My own learning largely mirrored Mark Crilley's comic book on drawing. Which is why I based this book's steps largely on his book. Look up "The Drawing Lesson". DeviantArt introduced me to various artists like Benedickbana, Robotpencil (Anthony Jones), BrandyRosa, EdensGarbage, groble63, ilovepumpkin2014, avvart, aenaluck, superschool48, RinaAshe, and Artofsade. Thanks people.

# PROLOGUE

This book was initially conceived as a record of my own learning journey. It morphed as I believe it is more useful to write in a manner that will help others.

Now walk with me. Those who wish to draw confidently will find that the book has various nuggets of wisdom. I might have learned these the hard way, but you can learn from my hiccups to accelerate towards confidence.

You do not need to own a computer nor even a phone, just plain old pencil and paper will suffice for drawing...but it helps to do so digitally. Tell you why in the first chapter.

This book detours regularly to show you how I draw using my chosen tools, Microsoft Surface Pro and Autodesk Sketchbook Pro. These are purely my preferences, and my wife would say my indulgence, at the expense of the family coffers. Love you. Smooch.

*Thanks @StettafireZero from DeviantArt community for the suggestion to write a prologue. It does help to anchor my thoughts and ensure I write for the right learner. See you on DeviantArt.*

# ABOUT A CONTRIBUTOR

Zen Teo Kin Hee
Zen is an award-winning photographer. His works can be found on https://www.instagram.com/zentkh/. Thanks for his constantly feeding me with inspirational photographs, I was able to learn how he composes his photos, and even use them as drawing references.

# CONTENTS

Begin with the end in mind                                    5

See shapes and then draw them                                 8

See shades and draw them                                     15

See shadows and ...                                          19

See negative space                                           25

Copy - creatively                                            29

Complex shapes                                               38

Composition                                                  43

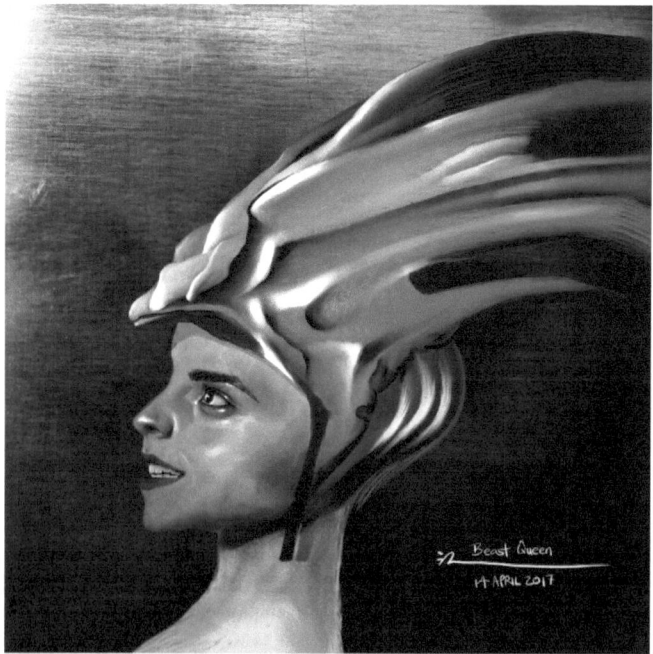

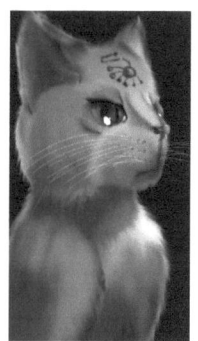

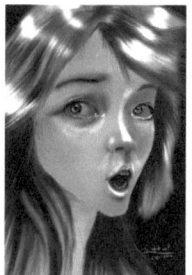

# Begin with the end in mind

If someone asks you to recommend them a drawing book, you would like them to thank you for recommending this one. So, my end in mind for this book, is for you to draw so well that someone beside you gets impressed, and asks you how you learned to draw. Shall we begin?

**To draw is to actually see first.**

You will find the next four chapters mostly about seeing. With your newfound eye, you can then train your hand to draw.

In time, you can learn from the masters, copy their work creatively, see like they do and arrange objects beautifully on your own masterpiece.

**Tools**

*"工欲善其事，必先利其器。", a Chinese saying.*
*If one wants to be good in a skill, one must sharpen the tools first.*

In learning to draw, there are many equipment that you can use. You need to know your options and eventually choose some. I will recommend this Autodesk Sketchbook Pro. It is simply convenient. No need to stock up on drawing pads, physical sketchbooks, pencils, pens, erasers, nor sharpeners. It runs on Microsoft Surface Pro, iPad, Android phone and even the iPhone!

Not that I never stocked up on traditional tools. I have loads of those. But eventually found that bringing just one tool really allowed me to travel light. It also suits my drawing habits, near electrical supply and creature comforts. :-P

Just to share, I drew with traditional drawing tools and experimented digitally. Started with Paper by Fiftythree on an iPad. Just finger painting. Then bought a simple passive stylus, rubber tipped. Using a stylus afforded more accuracy when doing detailed work. Then an Adonit Jot Pro stylus. Tried other hardware, like my Samsung Android phones, HP touchscreen laptops, HP Envy 27 touchscreen computer, and finally Microsoft Surface Pro. Switched to free trial version of Autodesk Sketchbook. I eventually paid the annual subscription to use the Pro version with unlimited layers and full features.

Options include these:

1. Traditional options
   a. Pencil and paper
   b. Pen and paper
   c. Watercolour and paper
   d. Watercolour pencil and paper
   e. Markers and paper
   f. Poster colour and paper
   g. Acrylic paint and paper
   h. Oils painting on paper
   i. Chalk on blackboard
   j. Mud on cave walls. Not that I tried.
   k. Stick in sand. I do this at the beach with my kids.
   l. Finger and coffee. I am not joking. Pictures drawn like this actually sell quite well.
2. Digital hardware options
   a. My finger on iPads and other touchscreen tablets
   b. Stylus and the same pads above
   c. Drawing tablet and computer
   d. Mouse and computer
   e. Drawing in Virtual Reality. This is the future.

The software available for digital options includes (in no particular order, and not limited to these only) :

| | | | |
|---|---|---|---|
| A. | Krita. Open source, | I. | Penultimate |
| B. | completely free option.Gimp. Also free! | J. | Art Set |
| | | K. | Autodesk Sketchbook Ink |
| C. | Adobe Photoshop | L. | ASketch |
| D. | Inkscape Illustrator. A different way to draw. All vector shapes. | M. | Comic Draw |
| | | N. | Pixelmator |
| | | O. | Autodesk Graphic |
| E. | Tux Paint | P. | Inkist |
| F. | Psyko Paint | Q. | Adobe Photoshop Sketch |
| G. | Sketch-Paint. Drawing on the internet itself! | R. | Adobe Illustrator Draw. Vectorised shapes. |
| H. | Autodesk Sketchbook Pro. They have a free trial too. The Pro annual subscription allows you to use the program on various platforms concurrently, from mobile phones, tablets to computers. | S. | Tayasui Sketches |
| | | T. | Inspire Pro |
| | | U. | Zen Brush |
| | | V. | Brushes Redux |
| | | W. | Sketch Club |
| | | X. | Procreate |
| | | Y. | ArtRage |
| | | Z. | Paper by Fiftythree |

Explore when you can, and eventually decide on which tool suits you best. Everyone is different, even joggers have preferences for different brands and makes of shoes. Artists are known for their individual uniqueness. Through experimentation, ups and downs, you will soon zoom in on a favourite tool, and perhaps use some others for various other purposes.

My basic requirements for any software are these: layers and a smudge brush.

Spend 10 minutes a day reading each chapter, then more 10 minutes another day to practise until you are ready for the next chapter. I squeeze in my 10 minutes daily when commuting to work, or while waiting for things to happen.

It has turned out to be interesting when strangers on trains peeped over and realised that I have been drawing them. Let us begin.

# See shapes and then draw them

**Objective**

You have mastered this chapter when you can confidently pick any object around you and see the basic shapes it contains in your mind's eye.

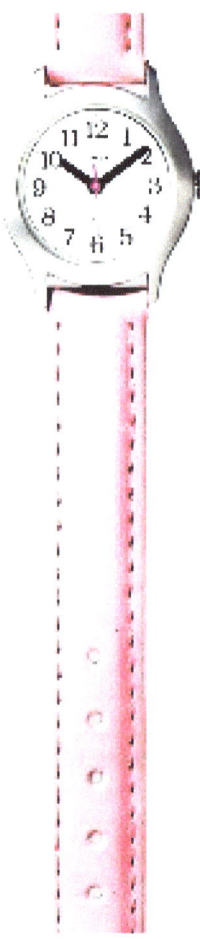

**Practise seeing**

When you see this watch, what shapes do you see? Do you see circles, rectangles and triangles?

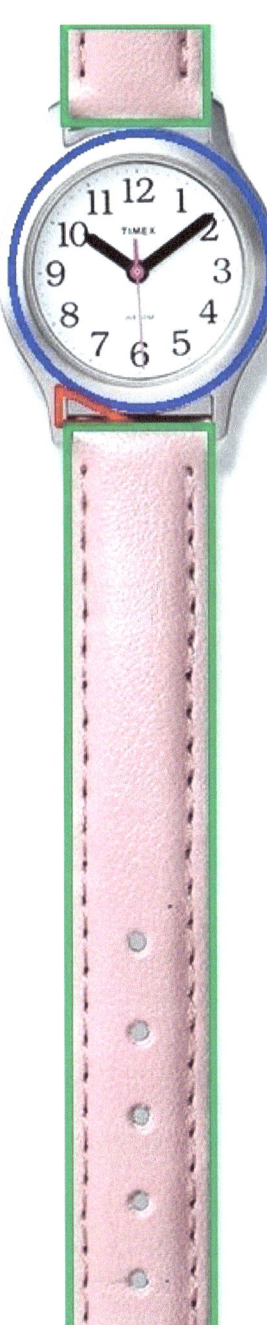

Do you see these basic shapes too?

**Practise seeing with your mind**
Without looking at your own watch, do you remember what shapes it is made up of?

**Practise**
Now take a good look at your own watch, and draw it with basic shapes first. This will be your first drawing practise.

**Look again**
Next, see if the shapes are sized correctly compared to the one beside it. Adjust accordingly.

**Look once again**
Now, see if you notice the spacing between shapes are correct. Adjust accordingly.

**Practise**

Take other simple objects that you have around you everyday, draw each with basic shapes. Again, check for relative sizes, and spacing between shapes.

**Technical Tip**

You can download Autodesk Sketchbook Pro from www.sketchbook.com and start with the free trial.

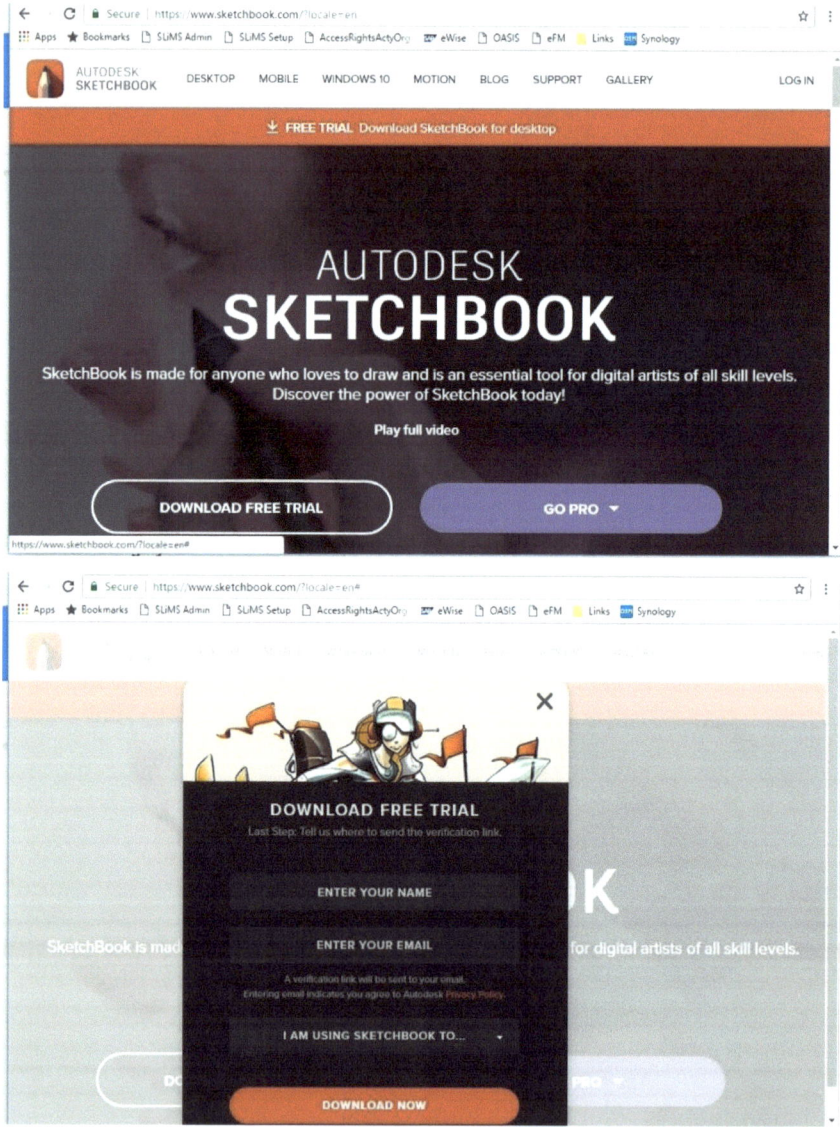

Give them your full name, email address, and download it onto your computer.

You can do the same for your Android, and your Apple iOS phones, including your tablets. Then start dabbling with your finger. If you have the luxury of a stylus (cue heavenly angels singing) then your experience in digital art creation will be off to a wonderful start.

In Sketchbook, you will see screens similar to this one below.

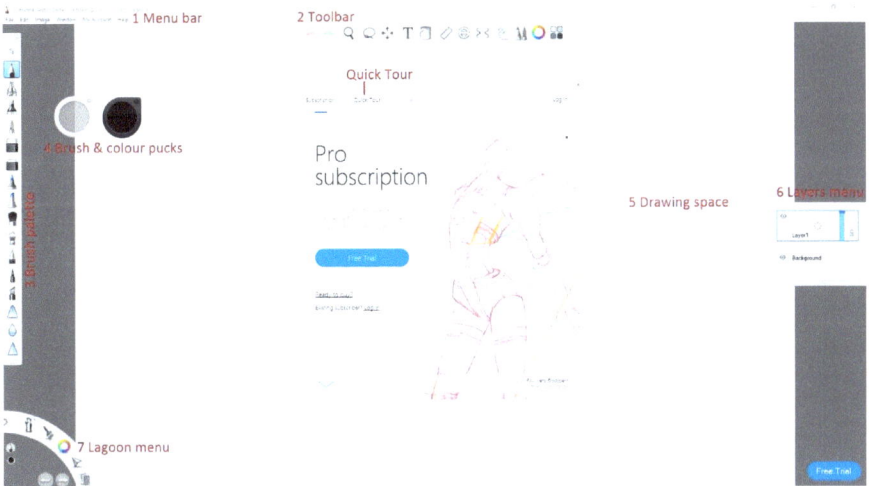

It is a great idea to click on the "Quick Tour" on that splash window, which does a great job of introducing you to the software.

Seven basic features visible immediately are described here:

| 1 | Menu bar | Functions for saving your work, among other things. |
|---|---|---|
| 2 | Toolbar | Provides drawing functions and ways to open up other floating menus. |
| 3 | Brush palette | Starting with the pencil, you will also find the hard and soft eraser there useful. |
| 4 | Brush & colour pucks | Quick ways to change brush sizes and change brush colours. |

| 5 | Drawing space | The white rectangle in the middle which you can pinch with 2 fingers to zoom and rotate. |
|---|---|---|
| 6 | Layers menu | There won't be many layers which you can add for the free trial, but usually enough for learning. |
| 7 | Lagoon menu | More quick ways to reach some functions. |

You will find that holding an icon, and sometimes dragging it around will bring up more options. After some time, you will discover the various shortcuts to reach your most commonly used features. Even the keyboard has some keys that let you reach your functions quickly. Personally I use these 3 shortcuts a lot:

- Ctrl-Z (⌘-Z on the Mac) which is "Undo"
- Ctrl-Y (⌘-Y on the Mac) which is "Redo"
- Ctrl-S (⌘-S on the Mac) which is "Save"

These are the few watches I drew, and saw more and more with each try..

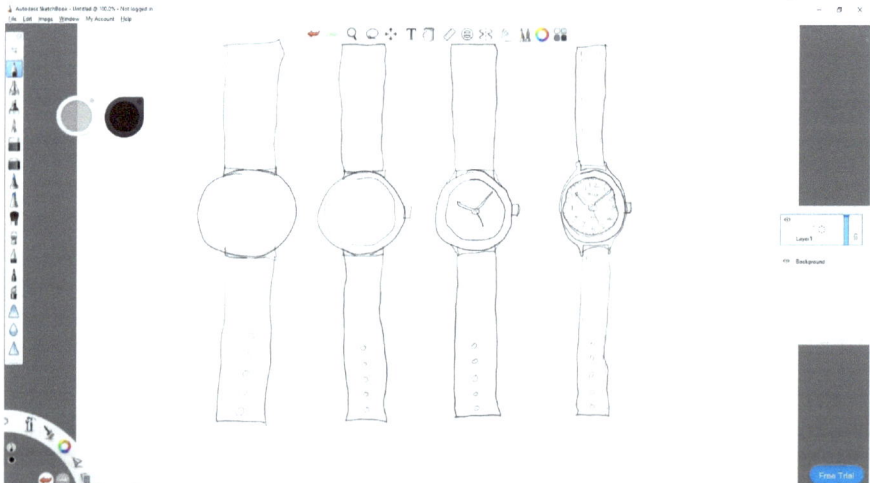

And some shapes are really small, like the dashes on the belt, the markings on the watch face. I am sure you can spend even more time slowly cleaning up the crooked lines, and spreading out small markings regularly until it looks exactly like the watch. Just be aware that a drawing is never complete until you and only you decide so. Learn to stop at a point where you are satisfied. A wise man (young man on YouTube actually) once shared that when learning, it is not quality that will help you grow, but quantity.

Once a while, when time permits, improve on your drawing until every dot is a perfect colour, but then, you might as well use a camera. But this last statement is of course my constant argument against drawing photo realistically all the time. Instead I prefer to let the mind wander and draw whatever it wants to have drawn. Most times, that surprised me pleasantly. Do try it.

Remember to save your work often. Give your drawing a good file name, so that you can find it back in future easily. You will eventually look through your progress, and amaze yourself at the speed of improvement with consistent practise.

*My son shared this quote with me,*
*"If you are persistent you will get it. If you are consistent you will keep it."*

## Technical Tip

For those 10 minute practises on the commute, I actually draw a lot on my handphone. From your App Stores, you can download Autodesk Sketchbook Pro onto your iOS, Android phone and tablets.

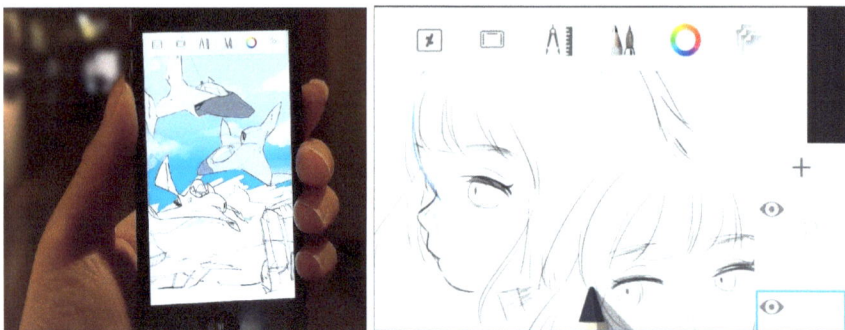

The usual pinch will zoom in and out. If pinch and then rotate, the whole image will also turn.

For the free download, only 3 or 4 layers are available, sometimes dependent on how big you decide the drawing surface should be since a bigger size takes up more phone memory.

Just explore it with your fingers.

# See shades and draw them

### Objective

You have mastered this chapter when you can tell which one of two points that you see is darker.

### Practise seeing

Which blobs are darker? The left ones are right. The right ones are not right. Have I confused you? Hahaha!

OK, lame joke. Forgive my having a little fun on my own.

The trick is to squint your eyes, or look through very small gaps between your fingers at each pair. Then you can see that those on the left are darker.

**Fun fact**: The toughest one is the last pair. Humans and a few other animals can see red. All others are blind to it.

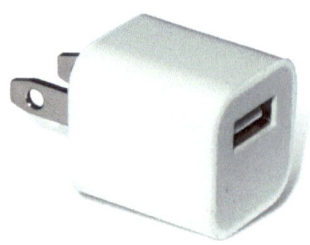

### Practise seeing

Now take an everyday object, any box-like object.

The one on my desk is a USB device charger.

In your mind, simplify it down to simple shapes.

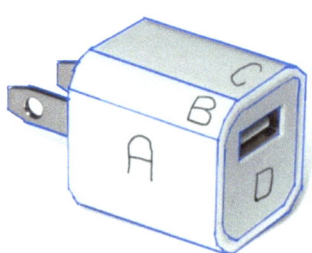

### Practise seeing more

Surface A is the lightest.

Do you agree that surfaces C and D are almost as dark?

Surface B has a curve and so it gets darker as darker as it moves from A to C.

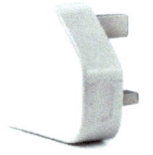

### Practise more

See other objects, identify the shapes, then the darkness of each compared to the rest. Identify areas which are like surface B.

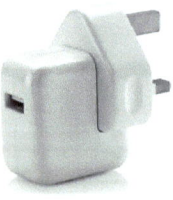

There are many ways to draw in a shade that is not quite black.

1. Gray coloured pencil.
2. HB pencil, and not a 8B one.
3. Water down the black water colour tube.
4. The obvious one would be to choose a shade of gray from the colour palette of Sketchbook.
5. Drawing lines to represent the curves.
6. Drawing dots closely or loosely.
7. Cross hatching.
8. Drawing another layer over previous ones.

Let me elaborate on a few. Please try different methods. I hope you become proficient in cross hatching and drawing more layers over previous ones.

### Drawing lines to represent curves

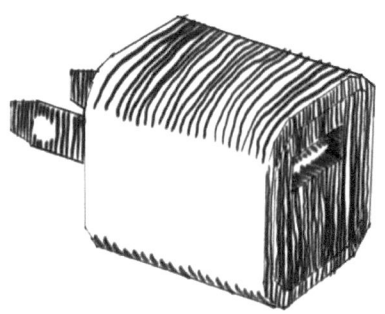

This just hints at the various darkness of each surface. The curves are easy to read with this method. Drawing tighter lines also gives the impression of a darker surface.

### Drawing dots closely or loosely

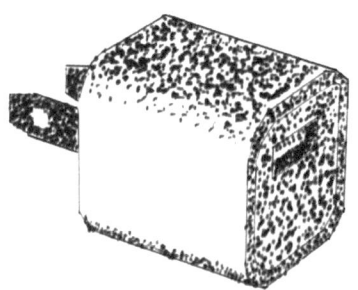

In the curved areas, the dots get closer as it gets darker.

## Cross hatching

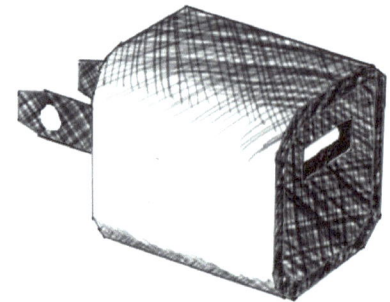

Drawing parallel lines in one direction. Then add a second direction to darken it. You can keep adding differently angled lines to achieve many different shades of gray.

## Drawing another layer over others

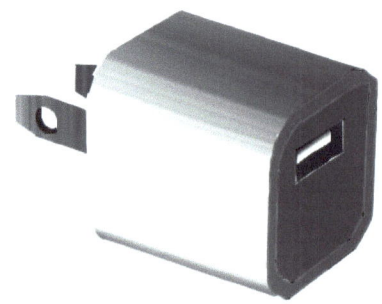

Shade a light layer. Then add another layer over it. Usually all in the same direction. With practise, this will be very evenly applied.

## Technical Tip

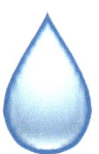

The "Blur" tool.

In Sketchbook, you will find that this brush allows you to quickly make the dots and the cross hatches become smooth.

Brush it over any rough spots, and you can quickly smoothen them.

## Fun use

It is also useful if you use it to touch up any rough skin. 美图秀秀 fans will know this well. It is an App for beautifying photos of faces.

## Practise

Try the 4 shading methods on simple objects you chose. In time, you will be able to say which one of any 2 given points is darker with just one look.

# See shadows and ...

### Objective

Once you notice the cast shadows of objects on the floor, it is a good start. When you notice that shadow dropped on another object, and onto other parts of itself, you would have mastered this chapter. Then you draw.

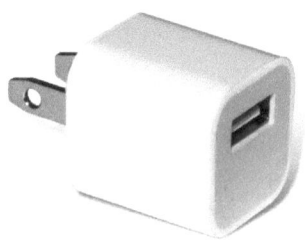

### Practise seeing it

Take another look at this object. Where is the shadow?

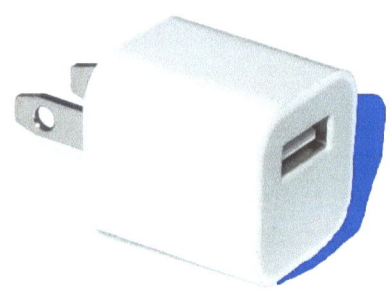

**Practise seeing more**

...than just this one

...than this one too

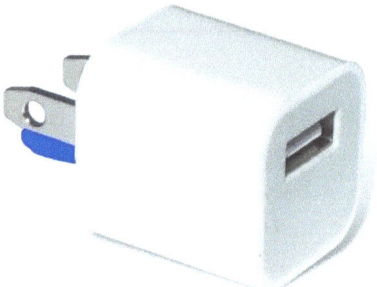

...even more

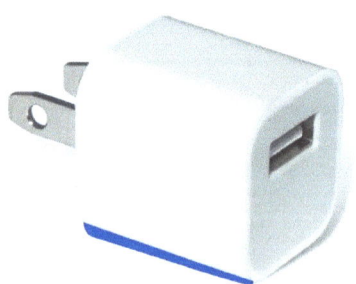

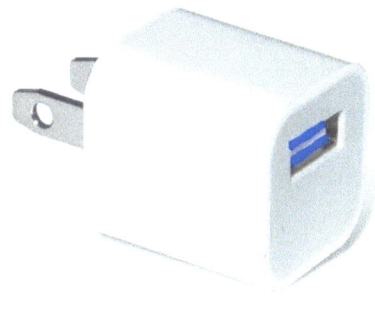

...and these are shadows

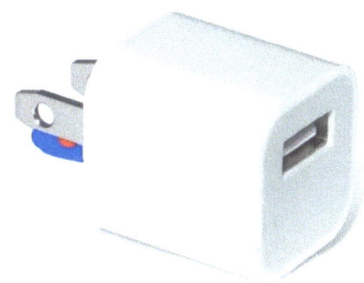

...you realise this red area is <u>not</u>. Yes, artists sees.

You can have the eye too!

**Practise seeing more**

Apply your new eye to objects around you. One by one. Then expand your eye to seeing even more complex scenes, identifying which shadow belong to which object.

**Practise drawing**

Now, pick an object similar to the example above, place it on a piece of white paper, and draw it, shadows included.

Something like this.

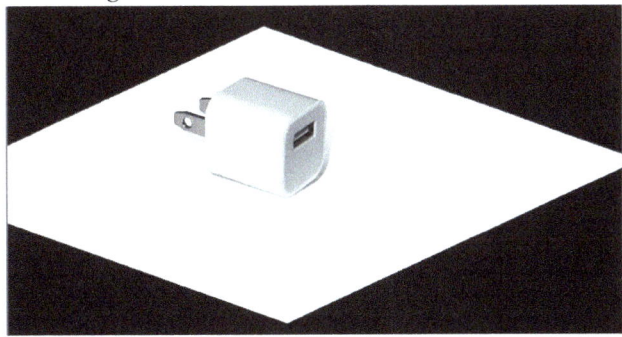

**Seeing tip**

A good way of seeing is to first seek out the area which is neither the brightest nor the darkest, right in the middle. We treat the shade of this area as the mid-tone. Once you see this shade, every other shade will either be lighter, or darker than this in comparison.

As an example, during cross-hatching, you can keep areas in mid-tones with three layers of hatching. All lighter areas will only have zero, one or two layers of hatching. The darker areas can have four, five or more layers.

I see these areas indicated by blue as mid-tones.

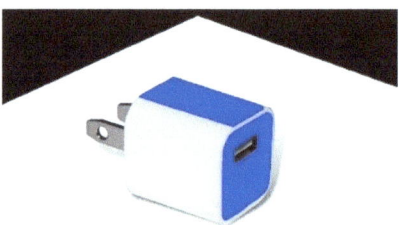

Cross hatch it in 3 directions.

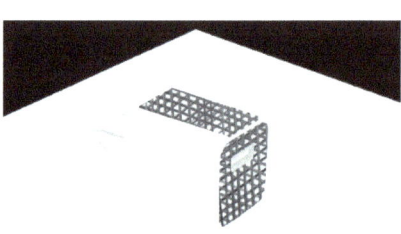

Cross hatch the next lighter areas in 2 directions.

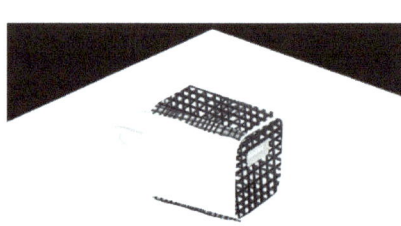

Cross hatch the even lighter area in just 1 direction.

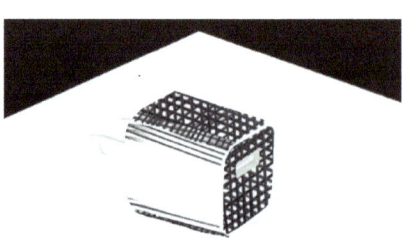

Now to seek out the darker areas, and cross hatch it in more directions as they get darker.

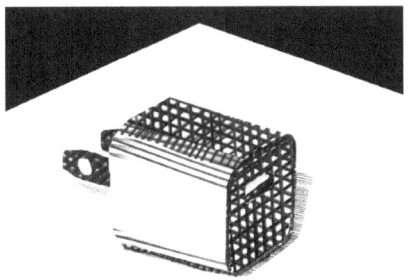

Oops. Almost forgot the shadows which are very light and so I lightly shaded that in.

You can probably do better than me. Especially if you cross hatch with lines closer to each other. I know you can do better than me.

**Practise drawing**

To practise, try drawing these pictures or other similar object arrangements of your own.

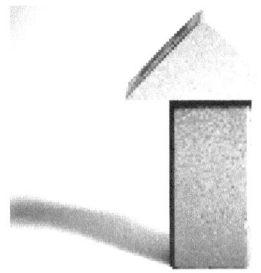

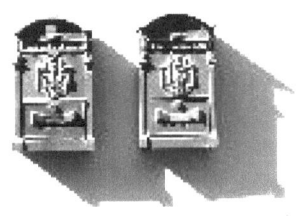

Go ahead and draw more now, until you can confidently draw the cast shadow of every object you see.

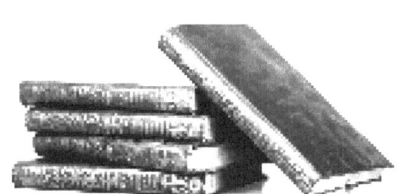

## Technical Tip

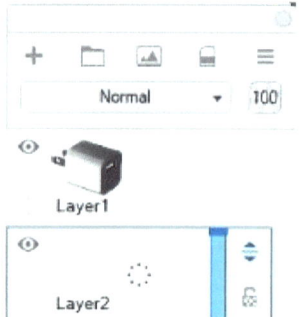

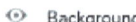

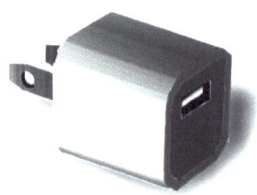

In many cases, the light source is muted, and shadows are just rough shapes, hardly clear lines. Try this in SketchBook. Add a layer below the object's layer.

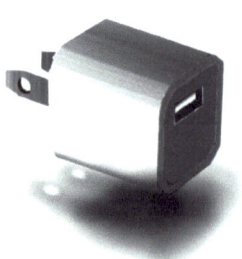

Then spray in the shadow as black. It will immediately anchor your object to the surface.

If you move the shadow away from the object's base, it will appear floating. Tada.

# See negative space

### Objective

When you can make use of negative space to help you improve your drawing, you would have mastered this chapter.

### Practise seeing

You can definitely shout out the shapes in this picture, down to the German word for newspapers on the cylinder. Challenge yourself to see the other shapes in between the letterboxes.

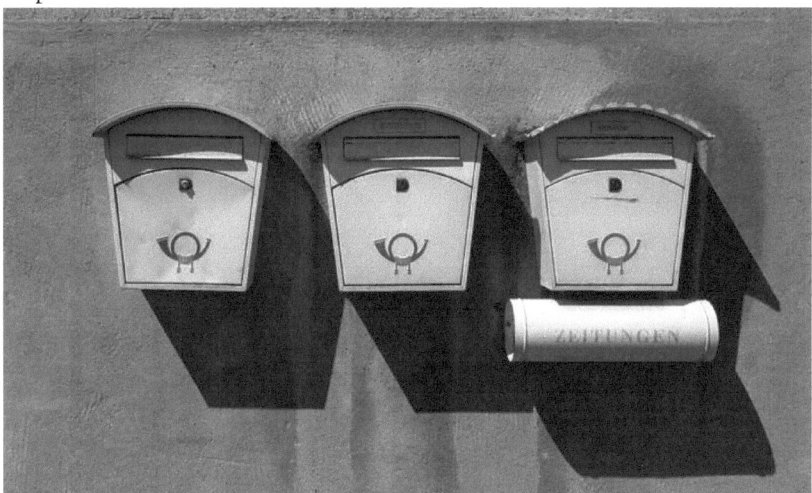

Do you see these shapes?

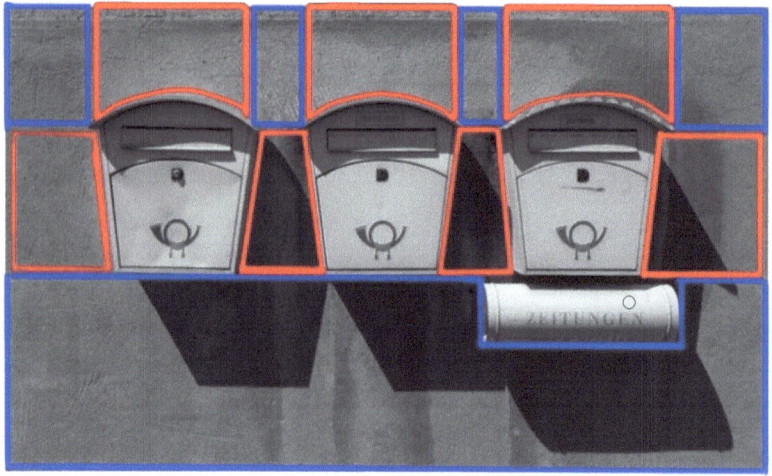

They fill up the negative space of your drawings.

Looking around you, and notice more of these shapes.

Now you can also ensure a few things:
1. Their sizes are correct.
2. Their positions relative to objects are correct.

That will help to ensure that the objects that you draw are even more accurately sized and positioned.

**Practise seeing more**

Can you see the negative spaces here?

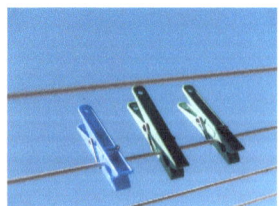 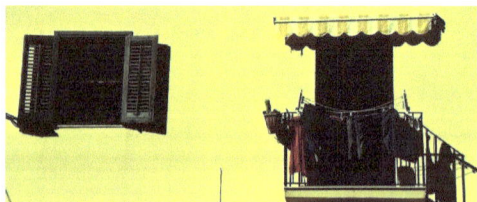

## Practise drawing these

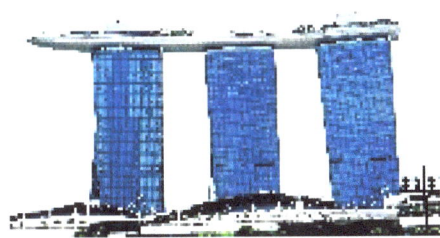 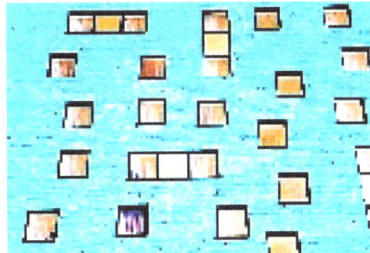

## Drawing tip

If you are simply drawing from these pictures, it is easy to use a ruler or even placing 1, 2 or more fingers between shapes, to help figure out the spacing.

When drawing from real life, you will have to use other methods. The simplest one, is to hold your pencil in the air, arm fully extended, and then using your thumb to mark the shape's height from the tip of your pencil.

Don't aim for perfect accuracy, as that equates to just taking a photograph, and it takes the fun away from this exercise. Just estimates will do. As an artist you can apply creative license to distort all you like.

I will not go into details, as you can find loads of such explanations elsewhere. This article is good:
http://www.drawinghowtodraw.com/stepbystepdrawinglessons/2010/01/how-to-find-measurements-proportions-and-angles-to-draw-with-pencil-thumb-method/

## Technical Tip

In Sketchbook Pro, you can use the ruler tool to help you draw radiating and parallel lines.

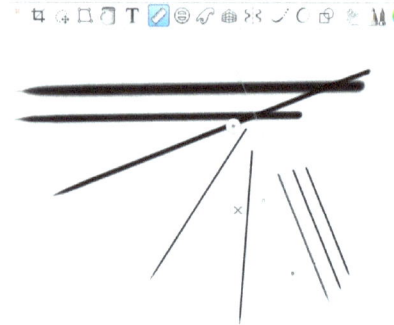

You can move the endpoints of the ruler to where you want. Then draw anywhere along the dotted line.

Then shift the ruler elsewhere if you want a parallel line drawn.

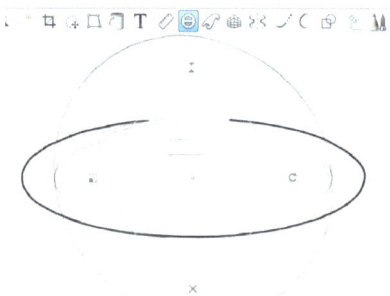

There is also an elliptical ruler which you can resize, rotate, and move to draw concentric circles and other shapes.

# Copy - creatively

## Objective

When you are able to see someone's drawing, and formulate in your mind how you can draw a similar one, you would have mastered this chapter.

## Practise seeing

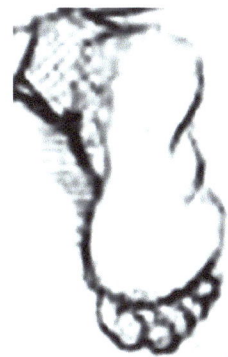

Michelangelo Buonarroti (1475-1564)
Can you see the many shapes he drew to make up this section of a picture?

Can you tell what shading method he used?

Can you spot the shadows?

Can you also spot the negative spaces?

Are you impressed with yourself that you can do all the above already? Go ahead, dance a bit. Give yourself a pat on the back.

(Source: https://www.pinterest.com/pin/231020655859507131/ )

**Practise seeing more**

See similar shapes in the other foot. Move up to see the shapes in the calf muscles, and thigh muscles. Eventually you will see how to place each section next to another, in appropriate positions and sizes. Take note of where he placed the shadows as well. You can see all that? Great job..

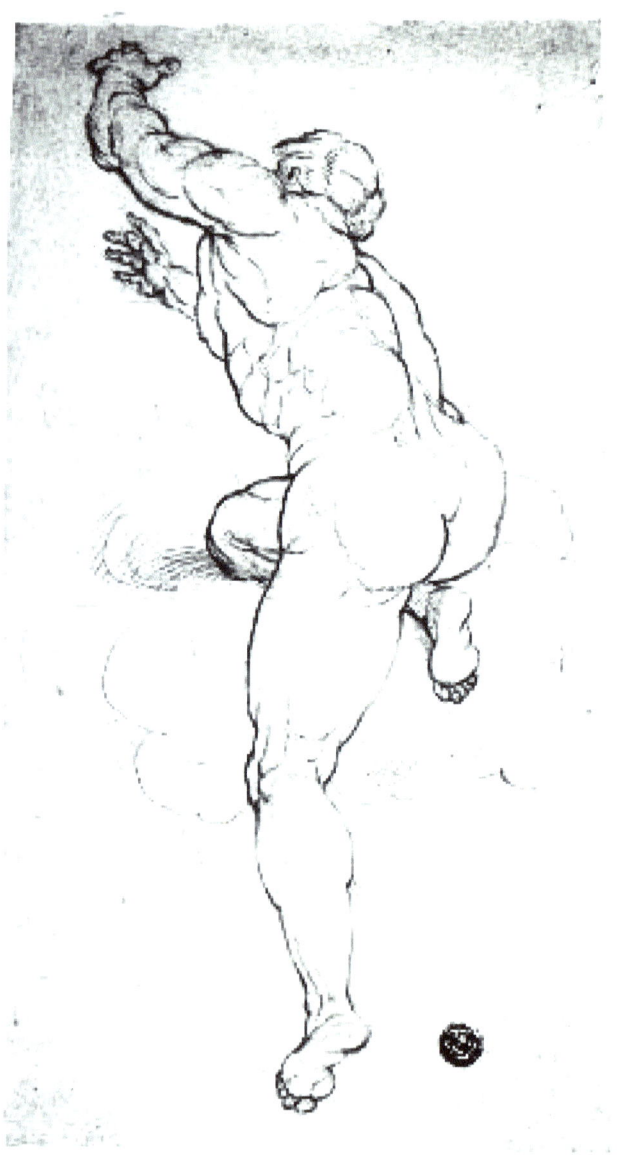

(Source: https://www.pinterest.com/pin/231020655859507131/ )

**Practise seeing more**

This is by Joseph Mallord William Turner (1775-1851). It is more challenging.

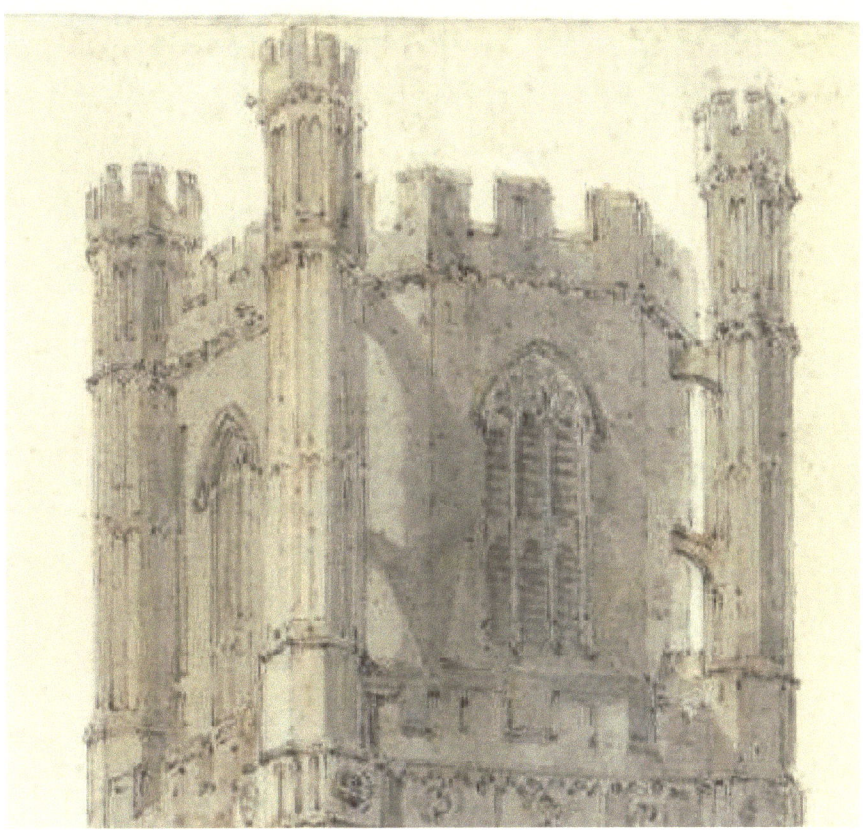

(Source: http://www.tate.org.uk/art/images/work/D/D00/D00352_10.jpg )

Can you see the shapes, very often repeated?
Can you see the shades?
Can you see the shadows?
Can you see the negative spaces?

The full picture is even more challenging, but can be understood and you observe window by window. Just take one small area at a time. This method allows you to slowly build up a drawing until you get the full picture. It is opposed to the general wisdom of drawing the big shapes first, then slowly getting into details. There is nothing wrong here. It is just an exercise to get you to see how each small part relates to its neighbour.

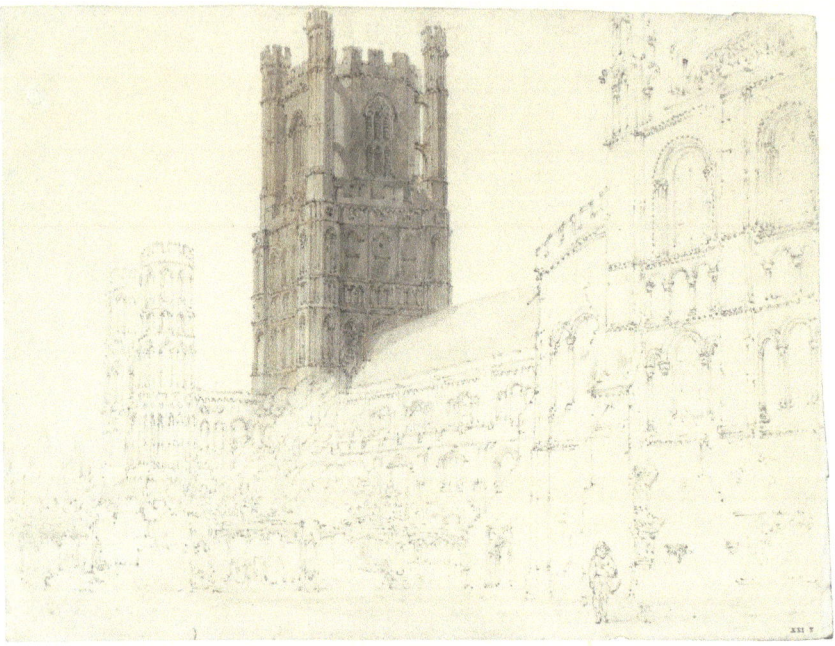

(Source: http://www.tate.org.uk/art/images/work/D/D00/D00352_10.jpg )

## Tip

Notice the human figure on the bottom right hand corner? Drawing a human being within pictures helps to let the viewer gauge the scale of the objects. You eye naturally makes comparison of everything drawn with the figure.

**Drawing tip**

Remember that it is great to find the mid-tone of a drawing, and start comparing other areas with it? Can you see how the whole paper's colour is the mid-tone? The Vittorre Carpaccio (1472-1526) only shaded the shadows and white chalked in the bright spots.

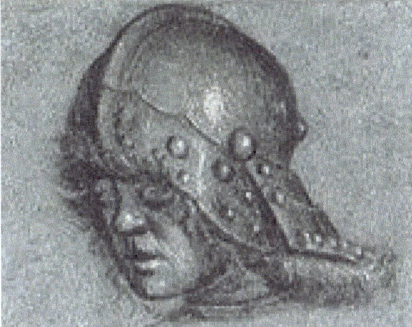

(Source: https://www.pinterest.com/alexeypavluts/vittore-carpaccio )

Such drawings make good use of the paper's colour as the mid-tone, saving lots of shading time. In olden days, this is probably a poor artist's way of using lower grade paper, very little charcoal and chalk.

This is the full drawing by Vittorre Carpaccio. Spot all the areas in shadow and highlights.

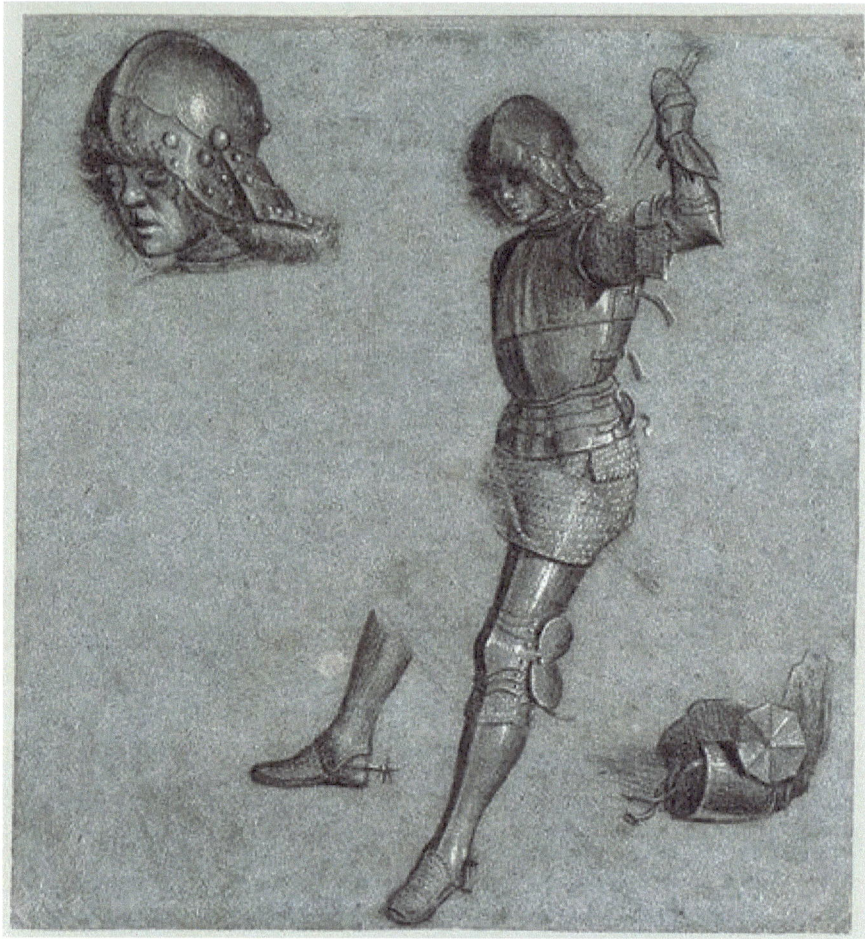

(Source: https://www.pinterest.com/alexeypavluts/vittore-carpaccio )

## Practise drawing

Consider using brown or grey paper. Then use only a black pencil to shade, and a white colour pencil to highlight (sparingly). Can you draw one of the objects on your table?

Suggested things to draw: eraser, a closed book, empty flower pot. Especially great if you can spot the brightest edges, and highlight it with white.

## Practise seeing

Just to train the eye, look at how these drawings make full use of the mid-tone of the paper to cover more ground quickly.

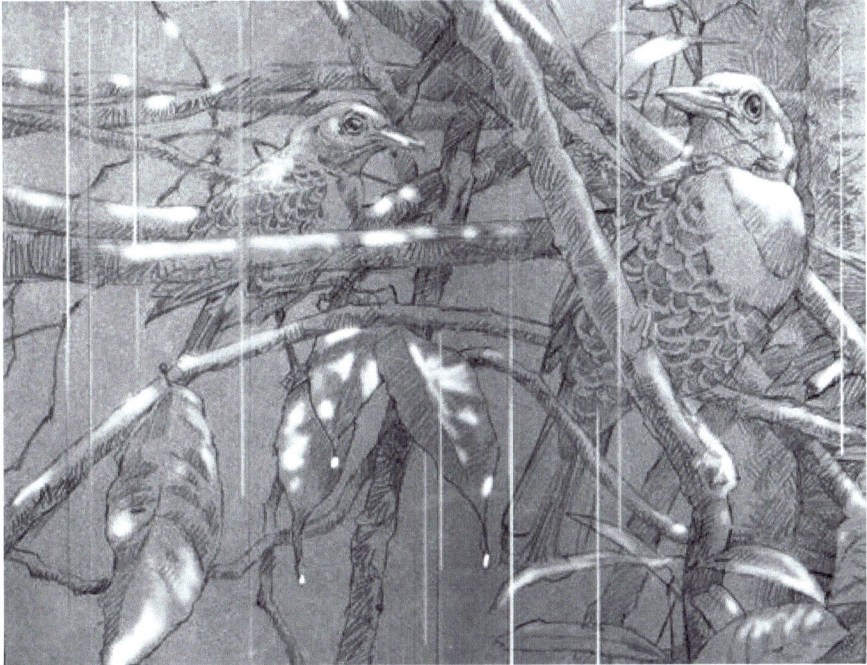

(Source:
https://drawingthemotmot.files.wordpress.com/2007/05/ocantbirdprogress2.jpg )

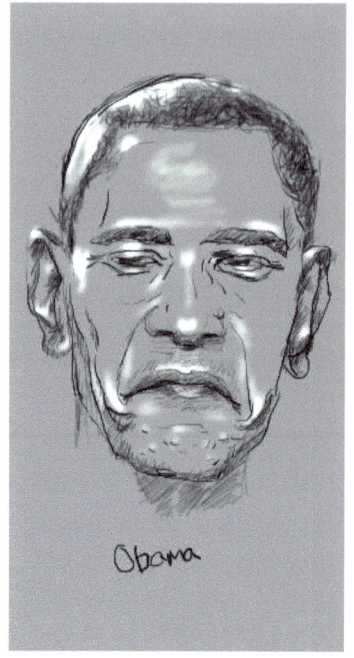
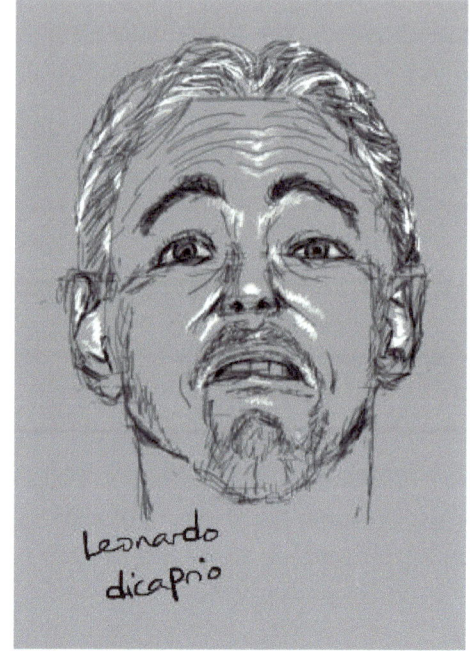

(Sources:
http://kangghee.deviantart.com/art/Caricatures-Obama-672471484,
http://kangghee.deviantart.com/art/Caricatures-Leonardo-672471155 )

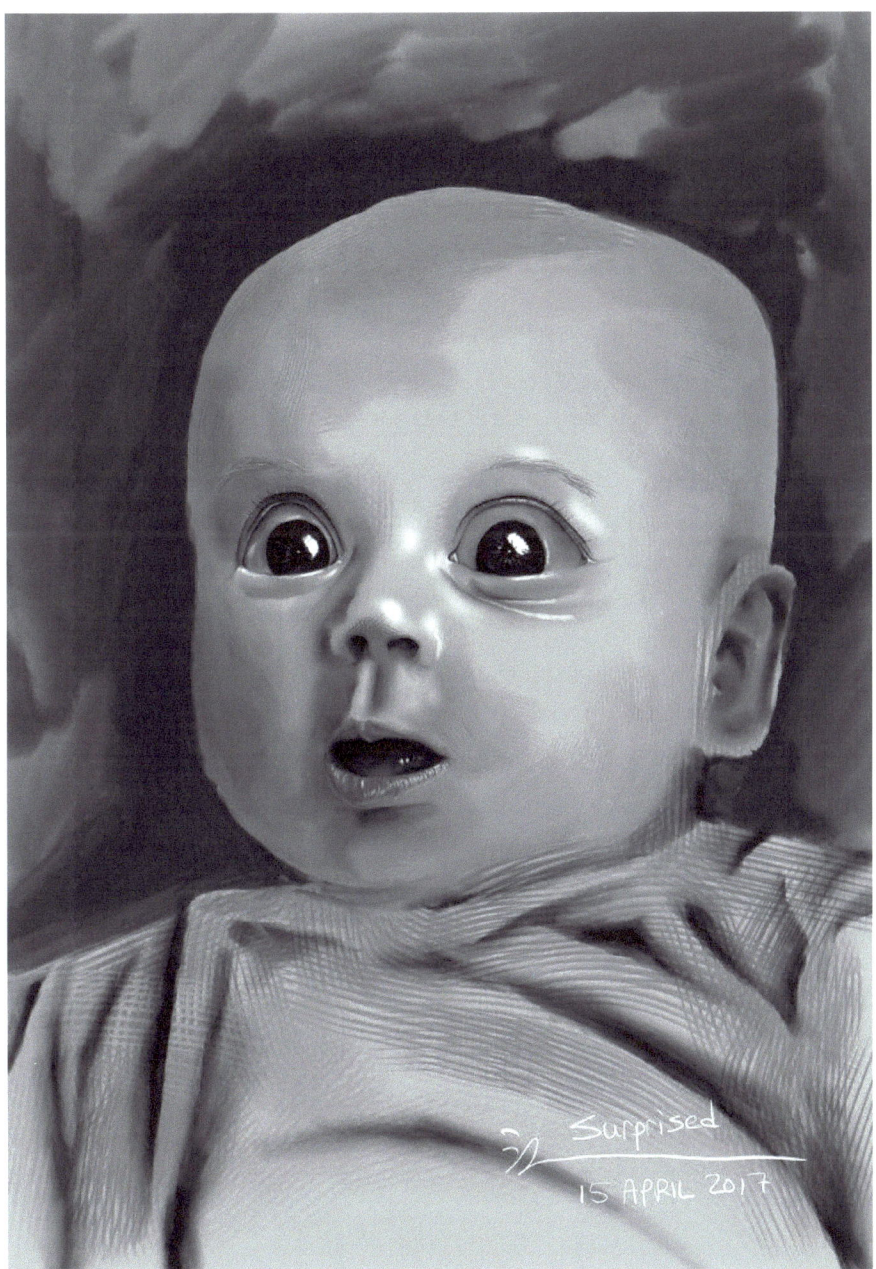

(Source: http://kangghee.deviantart.com/art/Baby-Surprised-675039399 )

# Complex shapes

**Objective**

Notice more complicated shapes made up of simple ones. Be able to compare those larger shapes against adjacent ones to get the sizes and positions right.

As you start to draw complicated objects, like Joseph Mallord William Turner's buildings, you will find it easier somewhat to merge simple shapes together. This makes it easier to compare adjacent complex shapes with each other, to gauge their sizes and positions better.

Better illustrated with examples as usual.

## Practise seeing

I have grouped some simple shapes into logical chunks. Such as the bike being the bike, the trailer by itself, the load and the ground.

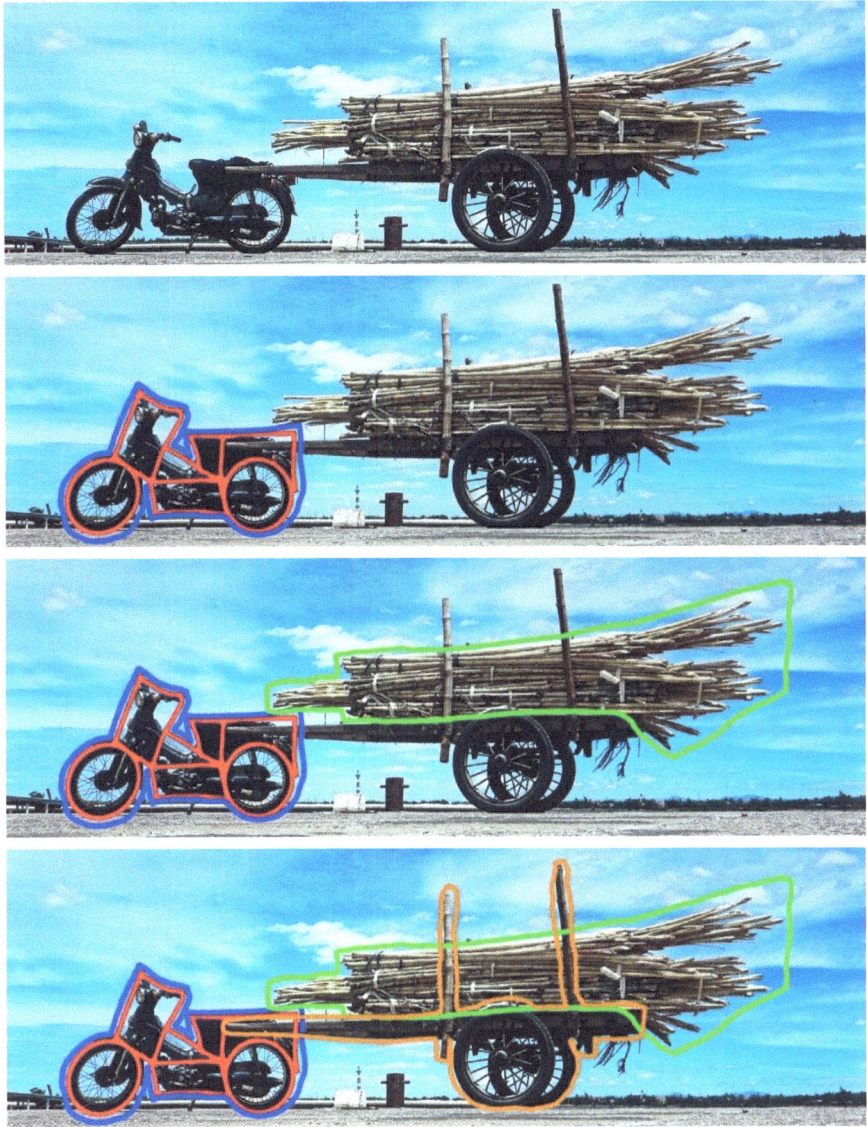

(Source: https://pixabay.com/en/transport-motorcycle-trailer-bamboo-642095/ )

This allows us to visually determine that the trailer's end is about one bike and one wheel more.

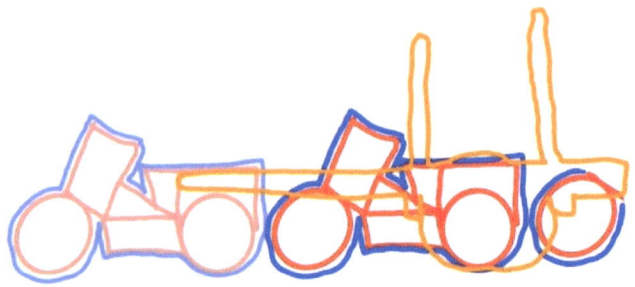

It also tells us that the two poles are more than 1 wheel apart.
A more accurate sketch is possible, like below.

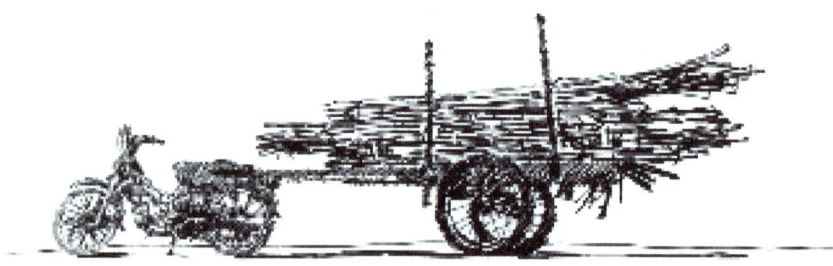

**Technical Tip**
Seeing all these allows us to draw in layers.

The top layer is actually the trailer. The bike and load can be on the same layer underneath. The layer below these is the ground. The bottom most layer is the sky. Then you can draw separately and even move them around to compare against each other.

These are my layers:

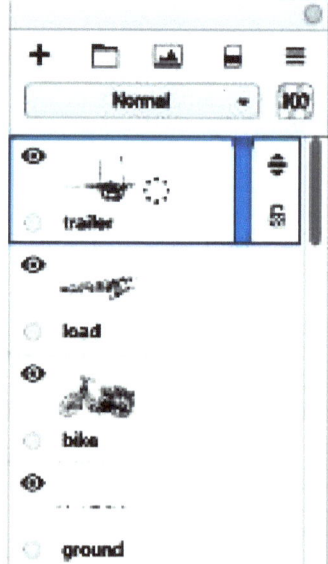

This way of seeing also helps you treat complex objects as just mergers of simpler shapes into blobs. Each blob can then be sized and positioned like any other shape.

**Practise on these**

Group, and then draw each one. Always considering the positions and sizes of each blob.

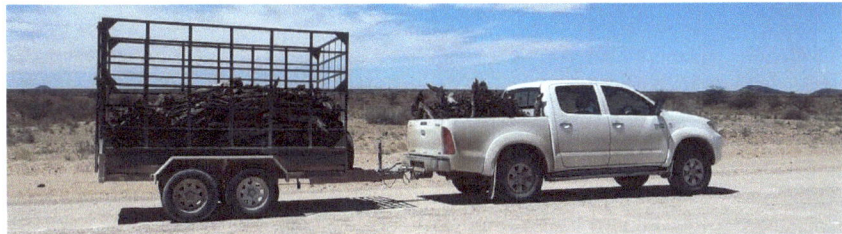

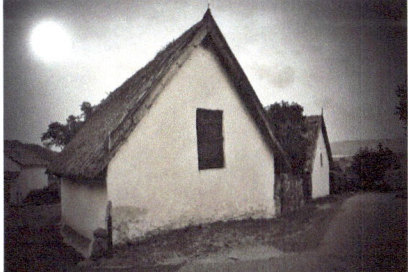 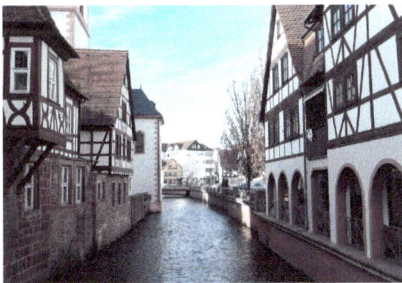

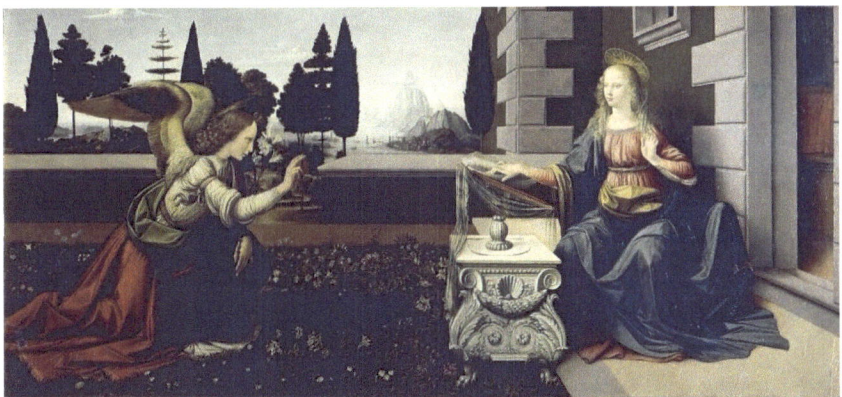

(Sources:
https://pixabay.com/en/car-trailer-carrying-wood-111812/,
https://pixabay.com/en/lake-balaton-szigliget-village-2109576/,
https://pixabay.com/en/erbach-odenwald-fachwerkh%C3%A4user-2136909/,
https://pixabay.com/en/the-annunciation-leonardo-da-vinci-1125149/ )

There are more out there which are beautiful but complicated. So you just have to learn to group many things together into larger blobs.

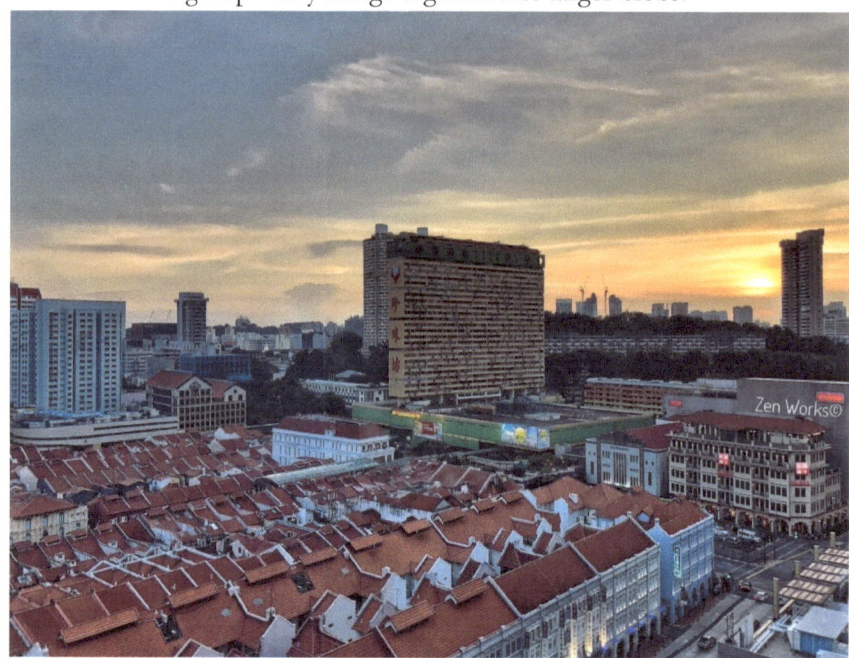

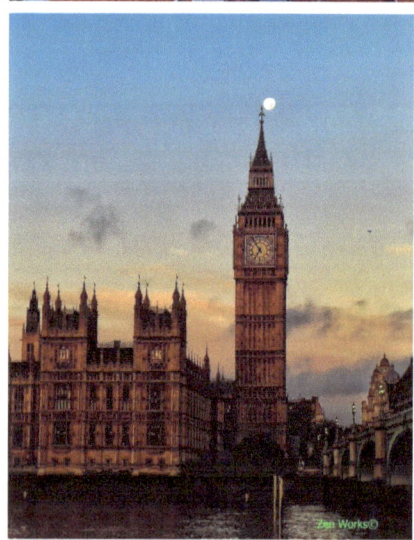

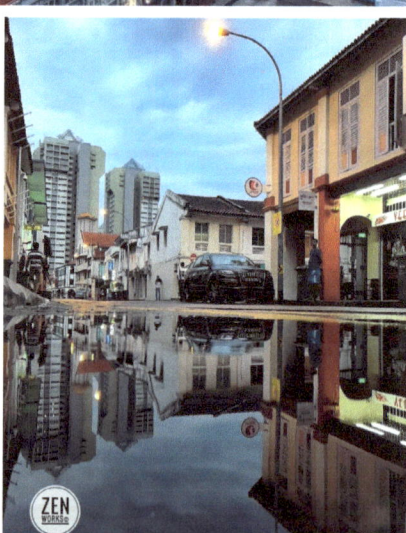

(Source: https://www.instagram.com/zentkh/ )

# Composition

**Objective**

You would have understood this chapter if you can spot how the artists lead your eyes around their drawing.

**Three Composition Techniques Which I Often Use**

**1. Greatest area of Contrast**

The simplest thing I always do, is to ensure that the area that I want focus on has the highest contrast. Basic contrast means it has white next to black, as opposed to varying shades of gray beside each other.

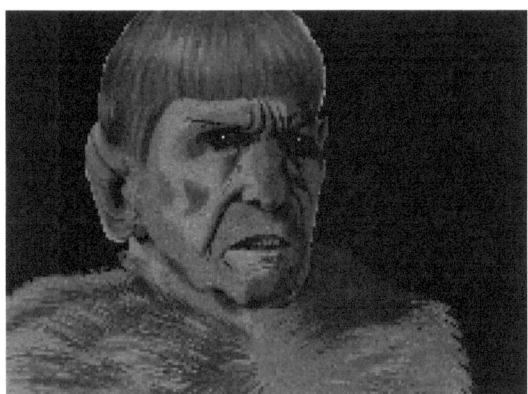

For my drawing of Spock, the only points with white on black are the eyes. So my eyes are immediately drawn there before radiating out along his wrinkles to look at other parts of the drawing.

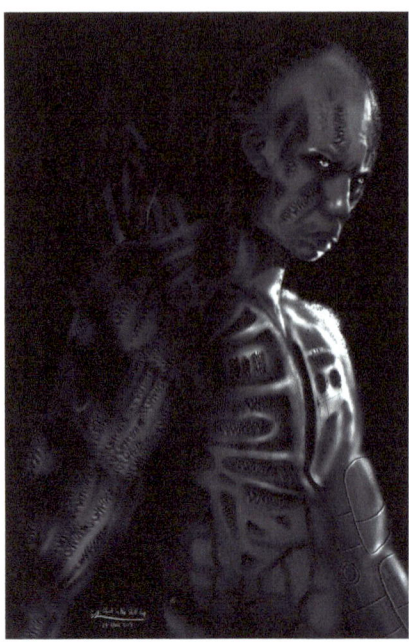

This drawing of mine was inspired by Ghost in the Shell. It is still the eyes which catches my attention, and then I look down at the bright shoulder before other darker parts.

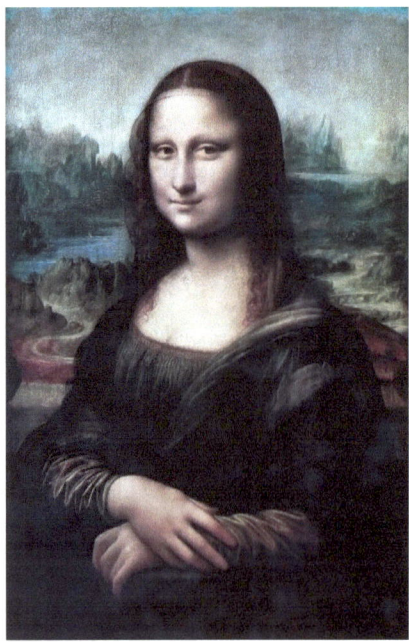

Even Leonardo da Vinci used this to great effect. Look at how we are drawn to the brightest part, the face contrasted by the dark eye balls.

## Tip

Contrast can be done with colours too. Putting complementary colours opposite each other will draw the eye there.

Complementary colours are on the opposite sides of a colour wheel, like green and red.

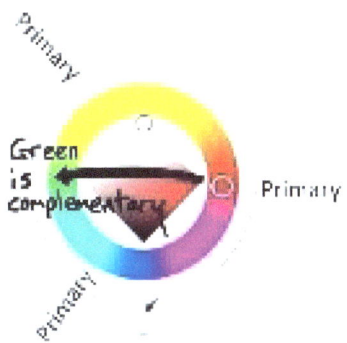

## 2. Law of Continuity

Take a look at this drawing by Edgar Germain Hilaire Degas (1834-1917). Starting with where you first glanced, do you feel the eye being drawn around the drawing?

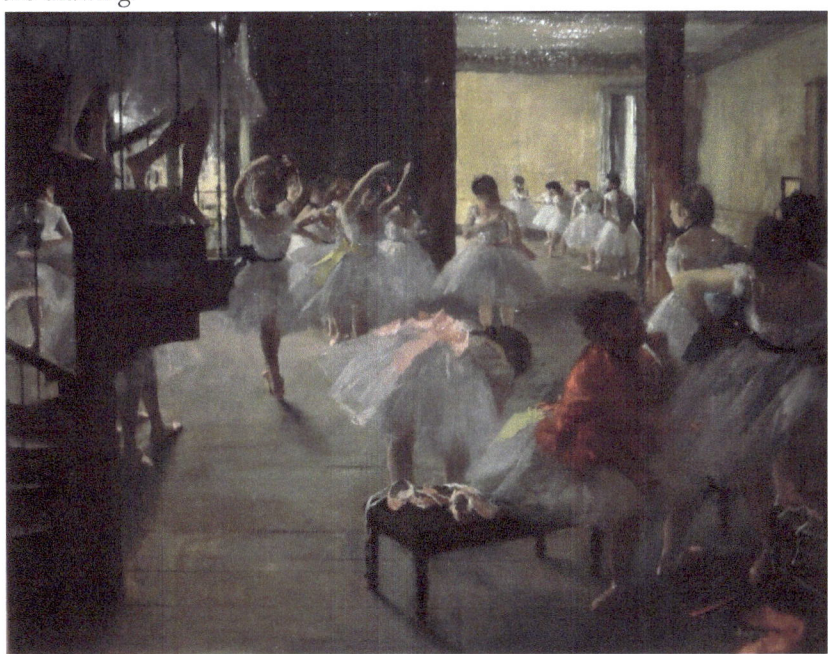

My eyes are drawn to the area with the highest contrast of bright window and dark wall.

Then continues along different areas of interest until I see every figure and action.

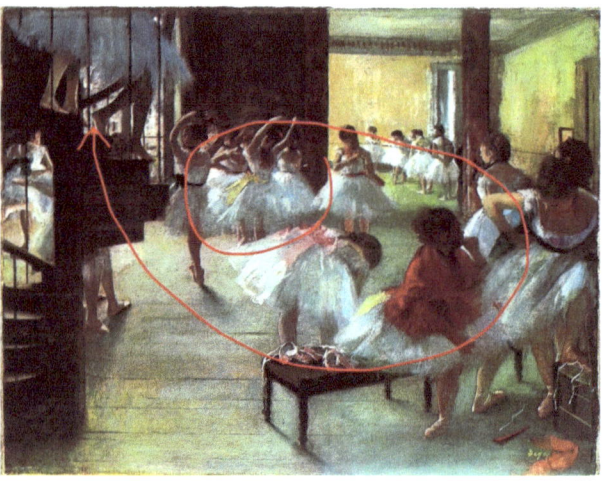

Take Vincent van Gogh's (1853-1890) Starry Night. Do you see how it leads the eye from point to point?

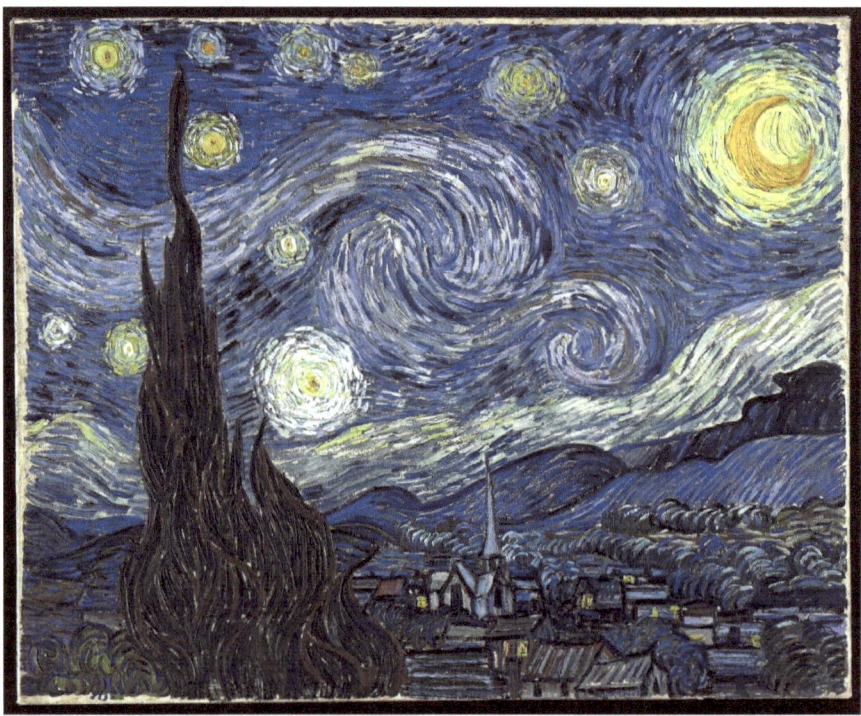

My eyes flow along this continuity.

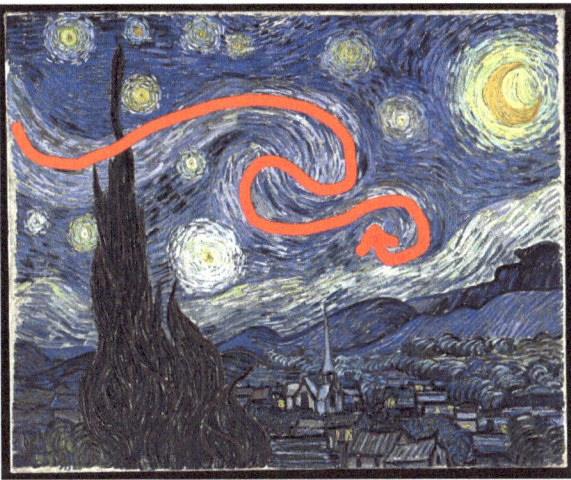

So there are ways to lead the eyes, be it using a cloud, interesting objects, a path, and even the direction a figure in your drawing is looking at.

### 3. Dynamic Symmetry

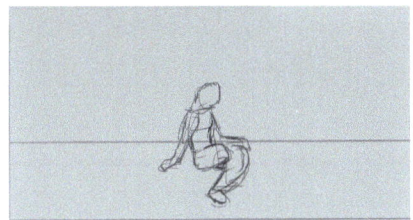

This figure looks nicely balanced in the center, just a bit boring unless the subject is really interesting to look at.

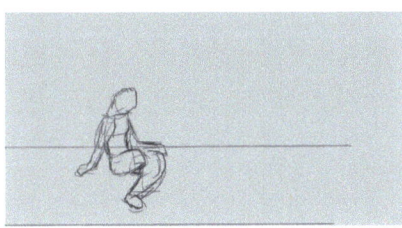

Moving subject to a side unsettles the drawing. The eye naturally looks at the figure, but does not travel to anywhere else. I might as well have placed it in the center.

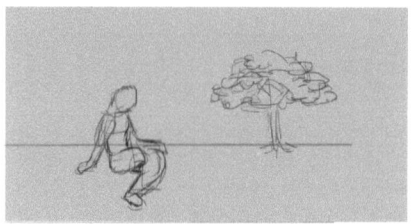

Adding a faraway tree to the right helps to balance the picture. Place that tree too far to the right won't feel good. I tried.

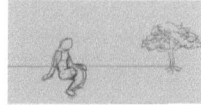

See what I mean?

The point is simply that for a drawing to feel balanced, the objects, the colours on all opposing sides would be best arranged to support each other.

And we are talking about all opposites, not just the center vertical line. Also the horizontal, the diagonals, and sometimes rotationally symmetrical if you are mathematically inclined.

## Counter-intuitive tip

From this, you will also learn one of the opposite points. To make the drawing feel out of balance, such as full of action, like all rolling down a slope, you can place them on a diagonal and all facing one side. That should give your viewers a tendency to lean to one side. They will feel the gravity that the drawn objects are experiencing.

**Further reading on Composition**

There are a lot of techniques for composing an interesting drawing. None of them are supreme over the others. But together they will help you build up a great piece. So read up on them separately. Just search on the internet or use the good old library.

Let me lightly touch on a few of these.

**Golden ratio**. Even nature follows this ratio, from seashells to where a tree sprouts branches. Find out how to place your objects along lines based on this ratio to get a natural balance.

**Weight**. Related to the topic on dynamic symmetry, it is possible to think of the image as a plate with the center balanced on your finger. Then making sure every object placed will help to keep this plate still balanced. Placing small objects further away from the center can actually help to balance heavy objects near the center.

**Grouping**. Related to the consideration of weight, you can also group some objects together to make them heavier, and thus alright to place them nearer the center.

**Ingredients**. When arranging for a drawing, you can use creative license to add or remove objects. Include only those that help to give meaning to the subject. For example, if you are painting a king's portrait, it will be great to add in objects that accentuate royalty. I remember one case where a French King wanted to demonstrate he is not quite one following tradition, his spire was drawn upside down. I assume he really held it upside down when posing.

**Perspectives**. There are whole books on this topic. In general, you will find it useful to know that drawings can be drawn in one-point, two-points, three points, fisheye perspectives and even a panoramic one.

**Rule of Thirds**. This one is famous but I will emphasize it least as there are really better ways of doing this, and a lot of literature that you can find online.

(Reference: https://petapixel.com/2016/01/30/10-myths-about-the-rule-of-thirds/ )

## Technical Tip

Perspective tool in Sketchbook Pro. If nothing else gets you to pay for the Pro edition, this feature would. I found it really a great time saver when sketching out realistic looking pieces with many objects in it. It basically allows you to place the vanishing points, even outside of the paper, and provides you with guidelines to draw along. Less than 5 minutes!

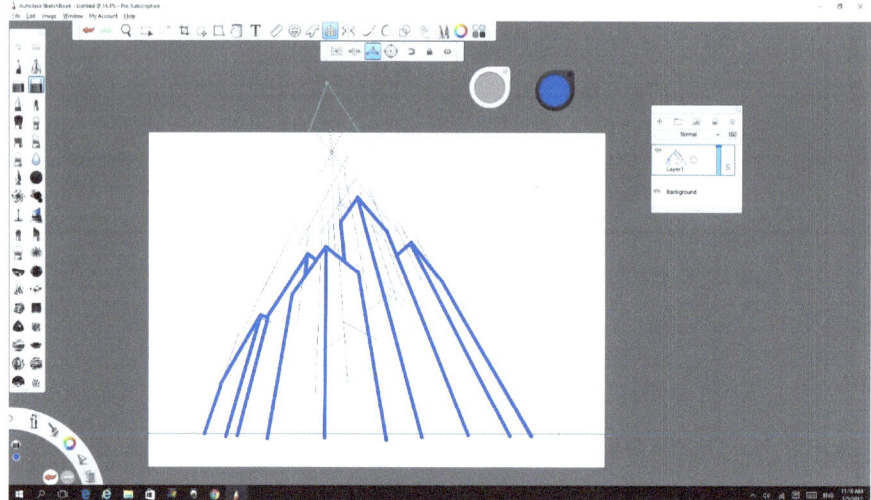

3 vanishing points shown here.
You can see a great video at https://youtu.be/ngLhGySVYLQ.

# PARTING WORDS

I had an experienced Sales Manager from my first job as Software Engineer for a Japanese MNC selling theodolites, those laser distance and angle measuring devices on tripods. Fabian's famous words were, "One eyed Jack is king in the Land of the Blind". He meant a product sells better even with one feature more than the rest.

After almost 20 years, I now understand it as having one skill more than the rest helps a lot.

Learn, practise often, a sketch in a corner of your book, on your phone, every day, on the commute, 10 minutes a day, and you will gain a skill. This one skill you will have that can help you be slightly different from your peers. Use it to help you communicate ideas. Use it to communicate love. Use it to zone out. Use it to invent.

Be the artist among your peers.

# ABOUT THE AUTHOR

Writing about myself is rather awkward, but here's a brief life story.

I am born in Singapore, 1971. The 70s were innocent years. Grandmothers still alive, cousins all kids and playing together. I was born into a one-room flat with a father who worked in the port, but was able to draw very well, in pencil and water colour too. My mother was great in class, but dropped out early to help support her family. This generation worked hard..

Mother insisted that she had enough money, and I need not worry about that. My younger sister was sensible enough to see through that charade. I conveniently believed it and grew up dreamily. Sis chose to complete her studies through a shorter path, to help support my studies getting a degree in Computer Science, from the National University of Singapore, in 1995.

Work life was fun and adventurous. Especially when coupled with marriage, and three boys. The excitement of life.

Work started for me as a Software Engineer. I ran our own robotics training partnership for 10 years, in parallel with point of sale software company, even developing and selling our golf ball dispensing systems which is a fully cashless, with smart cards storing monetary value. Went on to become IT Manager for China in Raffles Education Corporation (based in Shanghai), Solutions Architect in Singapore Management University (SMU), coaching student leaders in Office of Student Life (SMU), and supporting alumni in Office of Alumni Relations (SMU).

In between work, my passion in drawing was rekindled. Partly thanks to having laid my hands on iPads, touch-screen computers, the Microsoft Surface Pro, with a stylus, the Wacom drawing pad, and most importantly the Sketchbook Pro software.

After 600 drawings and through learning from great people on deviantart.com, behance.net, pinterest.com, artstation.com, youtube.com, patreon.com, pixiv.net, the extensive libraries in Singapore … this book was penned to help others who want to draw too.

## SOME THINGS TO SHARE WITH YOU

While I drew, I tried to record down the drawing steps for some of the works. Below are some that you can refer to and practise along.

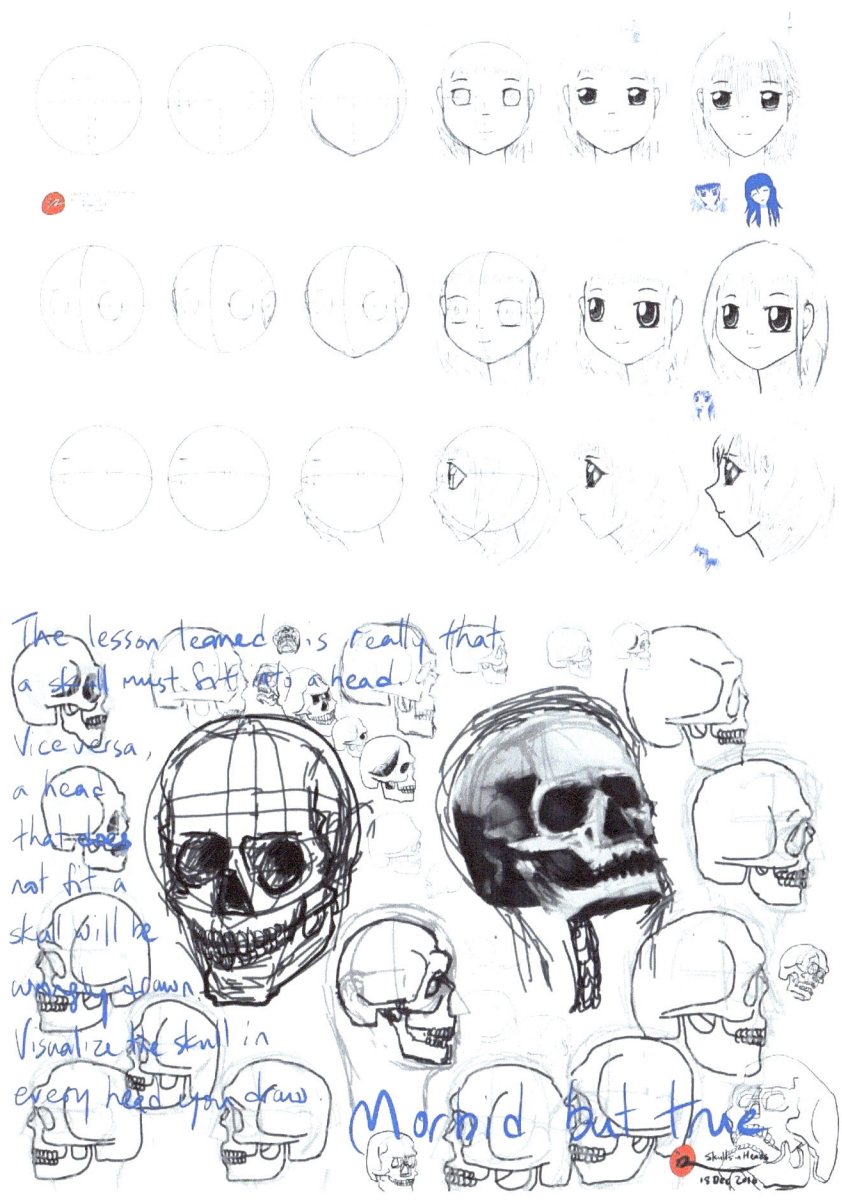

These next 4 are samples of what I was drawing a lot on the commute. I try to capture the faces I see, and sometimes adding or changing them just to keep it fun. There's actually a lot more, but mostly just scribbles.

Such practices are great for improving your confidence. Especially when the fellow passengers peer over and try to guess who you are drawing. When they can identify, you know you have drawn well.

If you are shy, just use your hand to cover your work. Most people will give you your privacy.

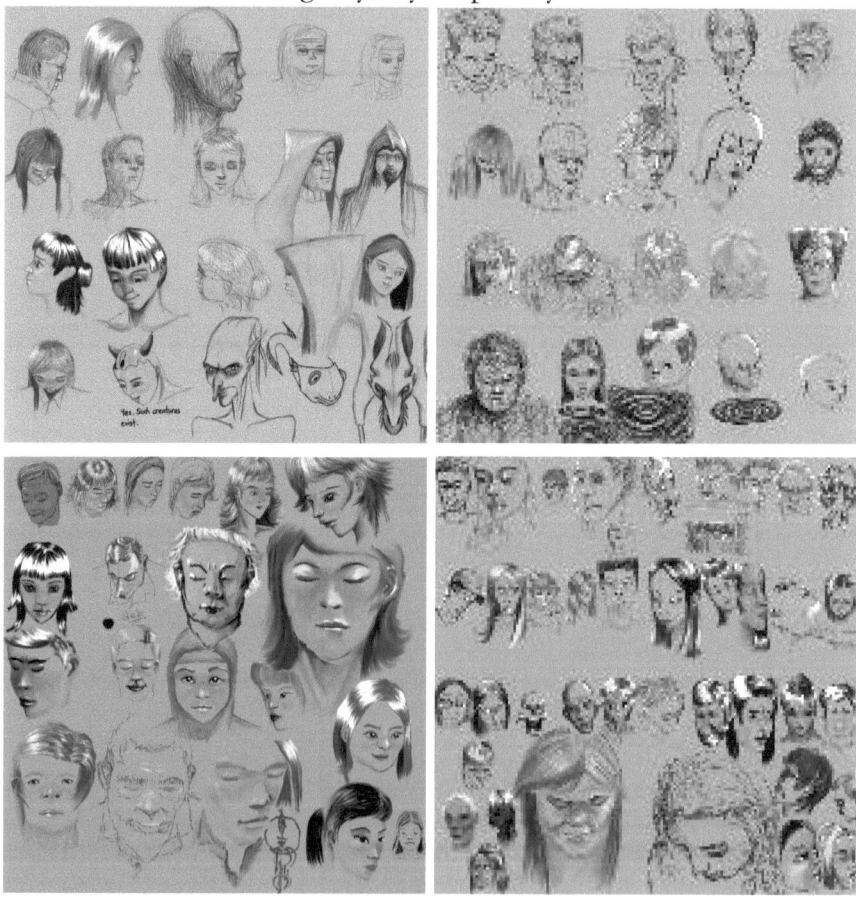

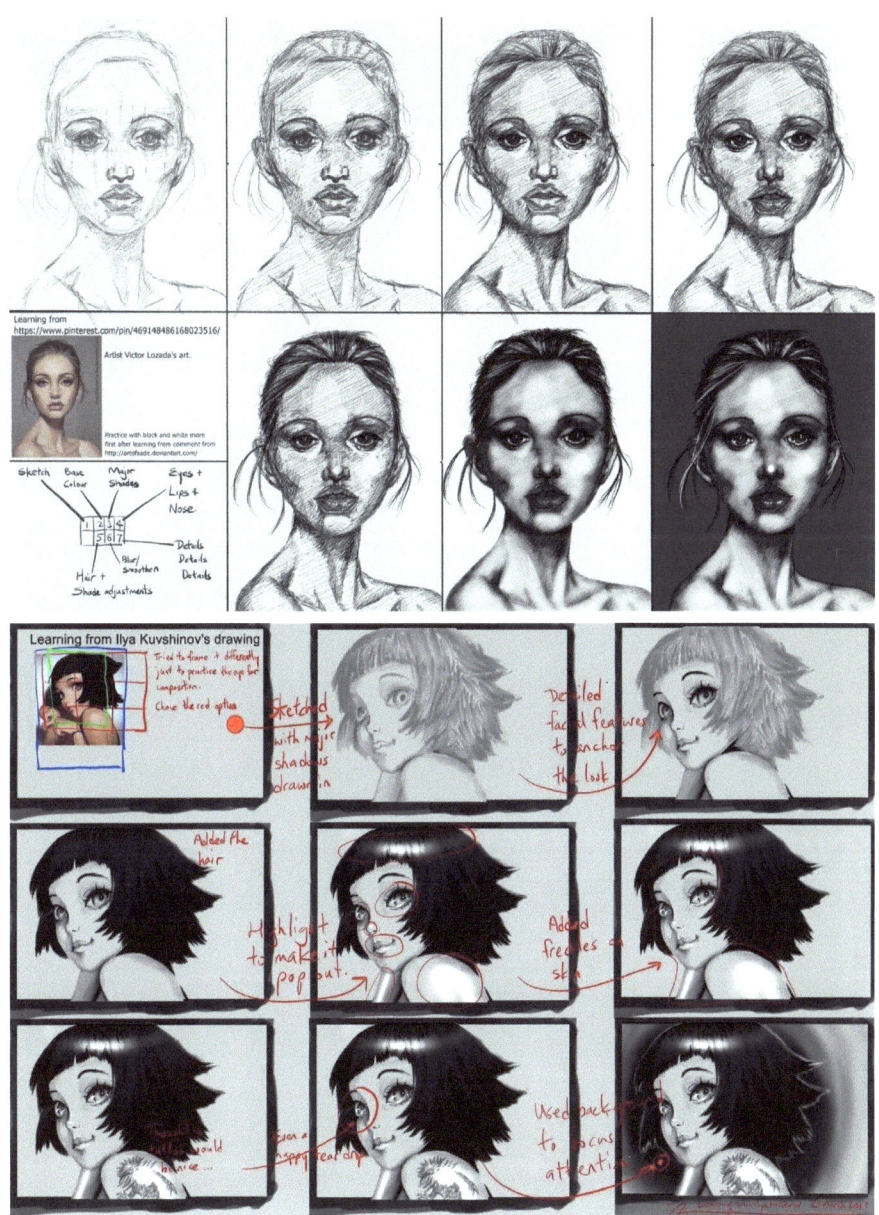

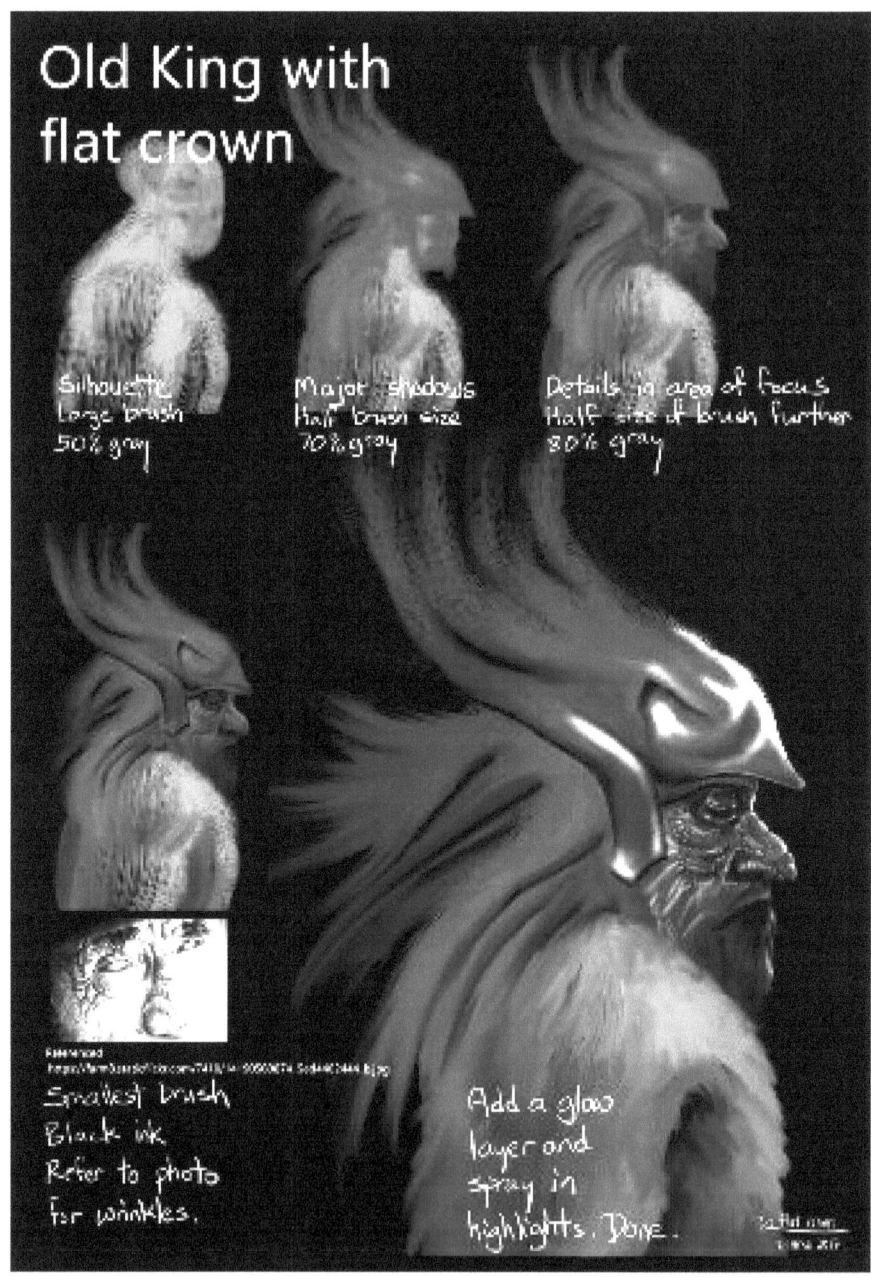

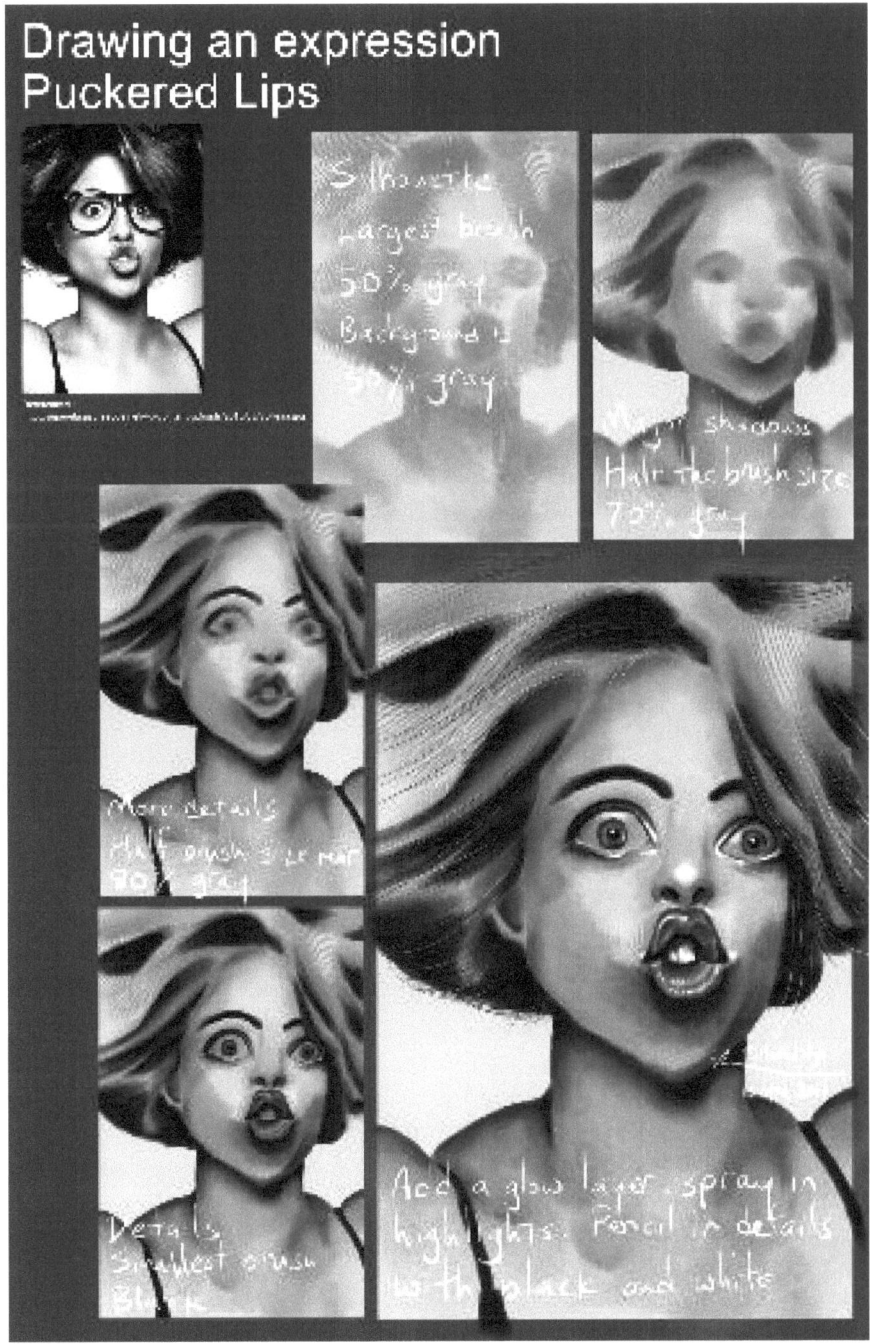

# REFERENCES

- Mark Crilley's book titled "The Drawing Lesson"
- Barrington Barber's book titled "Draw like the Masters"
- Community members and their drawings on websites like DeviantArt.com, ArtStation.com, Behance.net, Pixiv.net, and pinterest.com.
- Sketchbook.com for the many tutorials, samples and screenshots of their wonderful drawing software, the Autodesk Sketchbook Pro.

# HOW OTHERS HELPED ME WITH THIS BOOK

Before it was written...

StettafireZero from DeviantArt said,
"That sounds like a great idea:) Maybe you could have an intro talking about why the book was written or who it's for? (If any prior knowledge is required). That might make a good prologue." and I added that in.  It was a useful advise.

Amritpal Singh Sidhu, alumni of SMU said, "Hope to get a signed copy •  ❥. So did Lim Jierong, "1 book for me thanks". Love you guys for the support.

And 36 people encouraged me to do this when I posted about it on Facebook. Thanks people. I feel the love.

After it was written, these kind people took time to review and suggest changes and gave me their comments...

Soon Chuan.  Thanks for helping with the grammar checks!  Also appreciate your sharing with me on suggestions for promoting Art.

A few others who quietly suggested changes here and there.

Very importantly, this book would not have been published if this one person never published his own books, climbed the proverbial Mt. Everest first and showed me that it can be done...

Prof Khoo Hock Seng with a few books to his name.  His career spans many MNCs and he is currently teaching in the Singapore Management University.  I learned how to publish a book from him. A lot more about life through his years of guidance.  Since I was fifteen!  Thanks Prof.

www.ingramcontent.com/pod-product-compliance
Lightning Source LLC
Chambersburg PA
CBHW040815200526
45159CB00024B/2983